WORDPRESS DEVELOPMENT GUIDE

Build and Manage Websites with WordPress

THOMPSON CARTER

TABLE OF CONTENTS

Introduction

WordPress Development Guide: Build and Manage Websites with WordPress

Welcome to the ***WordPress Development Guide: Build and Manage Websites with WordPress***. Whether you're a complete beginner or an experienced developer looking to refine your skills, this book is designed to take you through the ins and outs of WordPress development in a way that's clear, jargon-free, and full of real-world examples. WordPress is the most popular content management system (CMS) in the world, powering over 40% of all websites on the internet. From simple blogs to complex e-commerce stores, WordPress offers an incredibly flexible and scalable platform that allows anyone to build a professional website with ease. But with so many options and features, it can be overwhelming for beginners to know where to start.

This guide is structured to provide a comprehensive yet accessible introduction to WordPress development. You'll learn not only how to build websites but also how to customize, optimize, and manage them effectively. Each chapter is focused on real-world applications, allowing you to gain practical knowledge that you can apply immediately, whether you are building a personal blog, a small business website, or an online store.

Why WordPress?

The first question most beginners ask when they hear about WordPress is, "Why should I use WordPress?" The answer lies in its simplicity, flexibility, and the vast ecosystem of themes, plugins, and resources available to users. WordPress powers everything from personal blogs to major corporate websites and even large online marketplaces. It's open-source, free to use, and continuously evolving, with an active community that is constantly building new tools and resources.

One of WordPress's most powerful features is its ability to scale with your needs. As you grow, you can enhance your site by installing plugins, changing themes, and using custom code to extend its functionality. Whether you're creating a basic site for your personal blog or a complex site with custom features for your business, WordPress provides all the tools to bring your ideas to life.

What Will You Learn?

This book will walk you through every step of WordPress development, breaking down the process into manageable tasks that you can easily follow. By the end of this guide, you will have:

- **A deep understanding of WordPress**: From installation to advanced customization, you'll gain a thorough understanding of how WordPress works under the hood.

- **The ability to build and customize websites**: You'll learn how to install WordPress, choose the right theme, configure plugins, create pages and posts, and customize your site's design to meet your specific needs.

- **Skills to manage and maintain a WordPress site**: Beyond just building a site, you'll learn how to optimize its performance, secure it from potential threats, and ensure it runs smoothly long after it's live.

- **Real-world examples**: Each chapter will include practical examples and step-by-step instructions that demonstrate how to implement the concepts you've learned. You'll walk through the process of building a site, customizing it, and optimizing it for performance and search engines.

Why This Book is Different

Unlike many technical books, this guide is focused on practical applications and clarity. It's designed to help you understand **why** you do certain tasks, not just **how** to do them. We'll avoid the heavy technical jargon and focus on real-world situations, ensuring that you can apply your knowledge immediately.

The **step-by-step approach** makes the book ideal for beginners, while the advanced sections will challenge more experienced developers to refine their skills. The emphasis on clear instructions and practical advice ensures that you'll learn at your own pace and feel confident building and managing your WordPress website by the end of the book.

Who Should Read This Book?

This book is for anyone who wants to build or manage a WordPress website. Whether you're a small business owner, a blogger, a designer, or a developer, this guide provides everything you need to get started or improve your WordPress skills. You'll benefit from this book if you:

- Are **new to WordPress** and want to build your first website.
- Want to **expand your knowledge of WordPress development** beyond basic usage.
- Are a **business owner or marketer** who wants to manage your own site and improve its performance.
- Want to **build custom WordPress themes and plugins** or dive into advanced WordPress development.
- Need to learn how to maintain a WordPress site for **security, performance, and SEO**.

How This Book is Organized

This book is divided into **20 chapters**, each focusing on a different aspect of WordPress development. Here's a brief look at how the chapters are organized:

1. **Introduction to WordPress Development**: Understanding WordPress and its ecosystem.
2. **Setting Up WordPress**: Installing WordPress locally and on your web hosting server.
3. **Understanding the WordPress Dashboard**: Navigating the Admin panel and site settings.
4. **Themes and Theme Customization**: Choosing and customizing WordPress themes.
5. **Installing and Configuring Plugins**: Adding functionality to your site with plugins.
6. **Creating Content with WordPress**: Building posts, pages, and using the block editor.
7. **Customizing Your Site with Widgets and Menus**: Adding widgets and creating navigation menus.
8. **Managing Media Files**: Uploading, organizing, and optimizing media.
9. **WordPress Users and Permissions**: Managing users, roles, and permissions.
10. **Building a Contact Form**: Using plugins to create and manage forms.

11. **WordPress Security Best Practices**: Keeping your site secure with essential plugins and practices.

12. **Optimizing WordPress for Speed**: Improving performance using caching and optimization tools.

13. **SEO for WordPress Websites**: Improving search engine rankings using on-page SEO techniques.

14. **E-Commerce with WooCommerce**: Setting up and managing an online store with WooCommerce.

15. **Building Custom WordPress Themes**: Developing custom themes from scratch.

16. **Introduction to WordPress Custom Post Types (CPT)**: Using custom post types to extend WordPress.

17. **Working with WordPress Custom Fields**: Adding and displaying custom fields and meta boxes.

18. **Introduction to WordPress REST API**: Interacting with WordPress using REST API.

19. **Troubleshooting WordPress**: Diagnosing and fixing common WordPress issues.

20. **WordPress Maintenance and Updates**: Best practices for maintaining and updating your WordPress site.

Each chapter contains **clear explanations, practical examples, and step-by-step instructions** to guide you through the process of learning and mastering WordPress development.

Conclusion

With its flexibility, ease of use, and expansive ecosystem, WordPress is the go-to platform for building and managing websites. This book is your complete guide to WordPress development, helping you navigate every step of the process— from setting up your site to customizing themes and plugins, securing your website, and optimizing it for speed and SEO. By the end of this guide, you'll be fully equipped to create professional, high-performance WordPress sites, manage them effectively, and keep them secure and up to date.

Let's get started and unlock the power of WordPress together!

Chapter 1: Introduction to WordPress Development

Overview of WordPress: What It Is, Why It's the Most Popular CMS

WordPress is a powerful content management system (CMS) that powers more than 40% of websites across the globe. It was initially launched in 2003 as a blogging platform, but over the years, it has evolved into a full-fledged CMS capable of managing all types of websites, from personal blogs to complex enterprise-level sites.

At its core, WordPress allows users to easily create, manage, and publish content online without needing advanced coding skills. It achieves this by providing a user-friendly interface with powerful customization options through themes, plugins, and widgets. One of the primary reasons for WordPress's popularity is its flexibility—users can build nearly any type of website with it, whether it's a blog, an e-commerce store, a portfolio, or a business website.

Key Features of WordPress:

- **Ease of Use**: WordPress offers an intuitive dashboard that allows anyone to get started, from beginners to advanced developers.

- **Customizability**: With thousands of themes and plugins, WordPress can be tailored to meet virtually any need.
- **SEO Friendly**: WordPress is built with search engines in mind, making it easier to optimize content for better rankings.
- **Scalability**: Whether you're managing a small blog or a large e-commerce platform, WordPress can scale with your business.

WordPress's open-source nature also means that it's free to use, with an active community of developers constantly improving and updating it.

Real-World Example: How Businesses Use WordPress for Their Websites

WordPress isn't just for bloggers or small personal websites; it's used by businesses of all sizes to build professional, functional websites. Some well-known companies have successfully leveraged WordPress to create dynamic, content-rich websites. Let's look at a few examples:

- **The Walt Disney Company**: Disney's official blog runs on WordPress, highlighting the platform's ability to handle high traffic and large amounts of content.

- **Sony Music**: The entertainment giant uses WordPress to manage its artist pages, news updates, and multimedia content.
- **Microsoft News**: The software titan uses WordPress to run its Microsoft News site, demonstrating WordPress's versatility for even large-scale media platforms.

Many small and medium-sized businesses (SMBs) use WordPress as a cost-effective solution for creating an online presence. Whether it's an online store powered by WooCommerce or a business site using a theme designed for professionals, WordPress provides the tools for every stage of business growth.

For example, a local bakery could use WordPress to build an online menu, a blog to share recipes, and a contact page with integrated Google Maps. A growing e-commerce business can start with a simple theme and gradually integrate more advanced features as the business expands.

Choosing WordPress for Your Website Project: When and Why WordPress Is the Best Option

While there are many CMS platforms available, WordPress stands out for several reasons. Here's why it's often the best choice for your website project:

1. **Cost-Effectiveness**: WordPress is free to use, and most themes and plugins are either free or available at an

affordable price. You only need to pay for hosting and any premium themes or plugins you choose.

2. **User-Friendliness**: WordPress's intuitive interface makes it easy for beginners to manage content, without needing advanced technical skills. Even if you have no prior experience in web development, you can launch and maintain a website using WordPress.

3. **Flexibility and Customization**: With thousands of themes and plugins, WordPress gives you the flexibility to customize your site to suit your business needs. From adding an online store to incorporating a booking system, WordPress makes it easy to add features to your website.

4. **SEO-Friendly**: WordPress is inherently optimized for search engines, and with the help of SEO plugins like Yoast SEO, it's even easier to improve your site's visibility on Google.

5. **Security and Support**: Regular updates, a large developer community, and plenty of resources make WordPress a secure and supported platform. If you encounter any issues, you can find help through forums, tutorials, and third-party services.

6. **Mobile Responsiveness**: Most WordPress themes are designed to be mobile-responsive, ensuring your website looks great and functions properly on smartphones and tablets.

7. **Extensive Community and Resources**: WordPress has a large, active community of developers, designers, and users, which means you can easily find resources, tutorials, and solutions for any problem you encounter.

When to Choose WordPress for Your Website Project

You should consider using WordPress for your website project if:

- **You need a cost-effective solution**: WordPress is free to use, and many themes and plugins are available at no charge or at a low cost.

- **You want an easy-to-manage site**: WordPress's intuitive dashboard allows you to manage content, update pages, and moderate comments with ease.

- **You plan to scale your site**: WordPress can easily scale as your business grows, whether you're adding new pages, products, or functionalities.

- **You need flexibility**: If you have specific design or functionality requirements, WordPress offers plenty of customization options.

- **You need an SEO-friendly website**: WordPress is built with SEO in mind and can be enhanced further with plugins to improve search engine rankings.

In conclusion, WordPress offers an all-in-one solution for building and managing websites, and it's the perfect choice for businesses, bloggers, and individuals looking to create a professional web presence. Whether you're starting a blog, launching a portfolio, or building an online store, WordPress provides the tools you need to succeed online.

This chapter serves as the foundational understanding of WordPress and sets the stage for diving deeper into its features, benefits, and practical applications in subsequent chapters.

Chapter 2: Setting Up WordPress

Installation on Local Server (XAMPP/MAMP): Step-by-Step Guide

Setting up WordPress on a local server environment is a great way to develop, test, and experiment with WordPress sites without affecting a live website. XAMPP (for Windows) and MAMP (for macOS) are popular local server software packages that bundle Apache, MySQL, and PHP in one easy-to-install package. Here's how you can set up WordPress on a local server:

Step 1: Install XAMPP (Windows) or MAMP (Mac)

- **For Windows (XAMPP)**:
    - Go to XAMPP's official website and download the latest version of XAMPP.
    - Launch the installer and follow the on-screen instructions to install XAMPP.
    - After installation, open the XAMPP Control Panel and start the Apache and MySQL services.

- **For Mac (MAMP)**:
    - Download MAMP from MAMP's website.
    - After the download, open the installer and follow the setup instructions.
    - Launch MAMP and start the Apache and MySQL servers.

Step 2: Download and Extract WordPress

- Go to the official WordPress.org website and download the latest version of WordPress.
- Extract the ZIP file to the web server directory:
  - **For XAMPP**: Navigate to C:\xampp\htdocs\ and create a new folder (e.g., mywordpress), then extract the WordPress files into this folder.
  - **For MAMP**: Navigate to Applications/MAMP/htdocs/ and create a new folder (e.g., mywordpress), then extract the WordPress files into this folder.

Step 3: Create a Database for WordPress

- Open your web browser and go to http://localhost/phpmyadmin/ (XAMPP) or http://localhost:8888/phpmyadmin/ (MAMP).
- In the phpMyAdmin interface, click on the "Databases" tab.
- Create a new database (e.g., wordpress_db) and select the collation as utf8_general_ci.

Step 4: Configure WordPress

- Open your browser and go to http://localhost/mywordpress/.
- WordPress will prompt you to configure the installation. Select the language, and then enter the following details:
  - **Database Name**: The name of the database you created earlier (e.g., wordpress_db).

- o **Username**: root (default for XAMPP and MAMP).
- o **Password**: Leave it blank (default for XAMPP), or use root (default for MAMP).
- o **Database Host**: localhost.
- o **Table Prefix**: Leave it as the default (wp_) unless you have a specific need for customization.

Step 5: Complete the Installation

- After entering the database details, click "Submit," and WordPress will run the installation process.
- Once completed, you'll be prompted to create an admin account. Provide a username, password, and email address.
- After clicking "Install WordPress," you can log in to the WordPress dashboard by going to http://localhost/mywordpress/wp-login.php.

Now you have a fully functional WordPress site running on your local server, where you can begin developing and experimenting with themes, plugins, and content.

Installing WordPress on Web Hosting: Setting Up on Shared Hosting and VPS

Once you've developed your WordPress site locally, the next step is to deploy it on a web hosting platform so that others can access it online. The process of installing WordPress on a live server is similar but involves some additional steps, depending on whether you're using shared hosting or a VPS.

Step 1: Choose a Web Hosting Provider

Select a hosting provider that supports WordPress. Popular hosting providers include Bluehost, SiteGround, and HostGator. Some web hosts offer one-click WordPress installation, while others require manual installation.

- **Shared Hosting**: In shared hosting, multiple websites share resources on a single server. It's typically affordable and easy to set up. Many providers offer managed WordPress hosting, which takes care of updates, backups, and security for you.
- **VPS (Virtual Private Server)**: A VPS offers more control and dedicated resources, making it suitable for websites with higher traffic. Setting up WordPress on a VPS is more complex, as it requires configuring the server environment yourself.

Step 2: Upload WordPress Files to Hosting

- **Using cPanel**:
  - Log in to your hosting account's cPanel (control panel).

- o Navigate to the "File Manager" and go to the public_html directory.
- o Upload the WordPress ZIP file that you downloaded earlier, then extract it in the public_html folder.
- o If you're installing WordPress into a subfolder (e.g., mywebsite), create the folder and upload the WordPress files there.

- **Using FTP**:
  - o Install an FTP client like FileZilla.
  - o Connect to your hosting account using the FTP credentials provided by your hosting provider.
  - o Upload the extracted WordPress files to the desired directory on your server.

Step 3: Create a Database on Your Hosting

- In cPanel, navigate to "MySQL Databases" and create a new database (e.g., wordpress_db).
- Create a database user and assign it to the database with full privileges.
- Note down the database name, username, and password as you'll need them during the WordPress configuration.

Step 4: Configure wp-config.php

- Open the wp-config.php file (found in the root of the WordPress installation) and edit the following lines with your database details:

php

```
define( 'DB_NAME', 'your_database_name' );
define( 'DB_USER', 'your_database_user' );
define( 'DB_PASSWORD', 'your_database_password' );
define( 'DB_HOST', 'localhost' );
```

- Save the file and upload it back to your hosting server.

Step 5: Run the WordPress Installation

- In your browser, navigate to your domain (e.g., http://yourdomain.com) to run the WordPress installation.
- Select your language, and on the next screen, enter the database details you configured earlier.
- Complete the installation by setting up your site title, admin username, password, and email address.

Once installation is complete, you can log in to your WordPress dashboard by going to http://yourdomain.com/wp-admin.

Real-World Example: Deploying a Simple WordPress Site on a Hosting Platform Like Bluehost

Bluehost is a popular hosting provider that offers an easy setup process for WordPress websites. Here's how you can deploy your WordPress site using Bluehost:

1. **Sign Up for Bluehost**: Go to the Bluehost website and select a hosting plan. Once you complete the sign-up process, you'll receive a confirmation email with your account details.

2. **Install WordPress with One-Click**: Bluehost offers a one-click WordPress installation. After logging into your Bluehost account, navigate to the "My Sites" section, click on "Create Site," and follow the prompts to install WordPress.

3. **Configure Your Site**: After installation, you'll be prompted to create an admin username, password, and email address. Bluehost will automatically configure the database for you.

4. **Access Your WordPress Dashboard**: Once the installation is complete, you can log into your WordPress dashboard by visiting http://yourdomain.com/wp-admin and begin customizing your site.

By using Bluehost, you benefit from an easy, streamlined setup with excellent support, making it a great option for beginners.

This chapter covers the essential steps to get WordPress up and running, whether you're working on a local environment for development or deploying your site live on a hosting platform. The next chapter will delve deeper into navigating the WordPress dashboard, customizing your site, and selecting the right theme for your project.

Chapter 3: Understanding the WordPress Dashboard

The WordPress Dashboard is the control center of your website, where you manage all aspects of your site. Whether you're a beginner or an experienced developer, understanding how to navigate and utilize the Dashboard is essential for effective WordPress management. In this chapter, we'll walk through the key sections of the WordPress Admin Panel, how to configure basic settings, and provide a real-world example of configuring your site for the first time.

Navigating the Admin Panel: Key Sections and What They Do

When you log into your WordPress site, you'll be presented with the Admin Panel (or Dashboard), which provides access to all the tools you need to manage your site. Here's an overview of the key sections you'll encounter:

1. **Dashboard (Home)**

o This is the default screen that you see when you log in. It provides an overview of your site's activity, recent comments, and any available updates.

o On the right side, you'll see a "Quick Draft" section where you can jot down ideas for posts, and "At a Glance," which gives a quick of your site's content.

2. **Posts**

o This section is used to manage blog posts. You can create new posts, categorize them, add tags, and organize your content.

o Under "Posts," you'll find:

  ▪ **All Posts**: A list of all published and draft posts.

  ▪ **Add New**: The option to create a new blog post.

  ▪ **Categories and Tags**: Used for organizing your posts.

3. **Media**

o The Media Library is where all your images, videos, and other files are stored. You can upload new media files, manage existing ones, and add them to your posts or pages.

o Under "Media," you can:

  ▪ **Library**: View all the files you've uploaded.

- **Add New**: Upload new images, videos, and other media.

4. **Pages**

   o This section allows you to create and manage static content such as your homepage, about page, contact page, etc.

   o Under "Pages," you can:

      - **All Pages**: A list of all your pages.

      - **Add New**: The option to create a new page.

5. **Comments**

   o This section shows all the comments left on your posts. You can approve, delete, or reply to comments here. This helps you manage user interaction on your site.

6. **Appearance**

   o This section is where you can change your site's look and feel. Key options include:

      - **Themes**: Choose and customize the WordPress theme for your site.

      - **Customize**: Access the WordPress Customizer to make real-time changes to your theme, such as colors, fonts, and layouts.

- **Widgets**: Add small content blocks (e.g., recent posts, archives) to your site's sidebar or footer.
- **Menus**: Create custom navigation menus for your site.

7. **Plugins**

   o WordPress plugins extend the functionality of your site. In the "Plugins" section, you can install, activate, deactivate, and update plugins.

   o You'll find the options:

   - **Installed Plugins**: Manage all the plugins you've installed.
   - **Add New**: Search and install new plugins to enhance your site.

8. **Users**

   o This section is where you manage the users of your WordPress site, including administrators, editors, authors, and subscribers. You can add new users, assign roles, and manage permissions.

   o Under "Users," you'll find:

   - **All Users**: View and manage your users.
   - **Add New**: Add new users to your site.

9. **Tools**

o This section includes various tools to help with managing content and site maintenance. For example:

- **Import/Export**: Import content from other platforms or export your WordPress content for backup.

- **Available Tools**: Includes miscellaneous tools that might be useful depending on plugins you have installed.

10. **Settings**

o The "Settings" section allows you to configure key settings for your site, such as site title, URL, and general configurations.

o Some important sub-sections under "Settings" include:

- **General**: Set the site title, tagline, WordPress address (URL), and email.

- **Writing**: Set default post categories, formats, and editorial options.

- **Reading**: Configure homepage settings, including how many posts are shown on the homepage.

- **Discussion**: Manage comment settings, including approval and moderation rules.

- **Media**: Set default image sizes for your media files.
- **Permalinks**: Define how the URLs of your posts, pages, and categories will appear.

Managing Settings: Site Title, Tagline, Permalinks, etc.

Configuring your WordPress settings is one of the first tasks you'll want to do when setting up a new site. Here's a detailed look at some essential settings:

1. **Site Title and Tagline**
   - Go to **Settings** → **General** to set your site title and tagline.
   - **Site Title**: This is the main name of your website, typically the brand or the name of your blog.
   - **Tagline**: This is a short description or slogan of your site. It appears in search engines and in some themes.

   Real-world Example: If you are setting up a website for a coffee shop, your site title might be "The Brewed Bean," and your tagline could be "Freshly Brewed Coffee, Right from the Heart."

2. **Permalinks**

○ Permalinks are the URLs of your posts and pages. By default, WordPress uses a URL structure that includes the post ID, which isn't SEO-friendly.

○ Go to **Settings → Permalinks** to configure a more user-friendly URL structure.

○ A good practice is to select the **Post name** option for permalinks, which results in clean URLs like http://yoursite.com/sample-post/.

Real-world Example: A blog post titled "10 Tips for Brewing the Perfect Cup of Coffee" would have the URL http://thebrewedbean.com/tips-for-perfect-coffee/.

3. **Timezone and Date Format**

○ Go to **Settings → General** to configure your time zone, date format, and time format. This ensures that your posts and comments reflect the correct local time.

○ Set the time zone to match your location or the location of your primary audience.

4. **Discussion Settings**

○ Go to **Settings → Discussion** to configure how comments will be handled on your site.

○ For example, you can choose whether comments require manual approval, if users can post comments without registering, and if you want to allow trackbacks and pingbacks.

- ○ **Real-world Example**: If you're running a blog with a lot of engagement, you might want to enable comment moderation to avoid spam.

Real-World Example: Configuring Your Site's Settings for the First Time

Let's say you've just launched a small business website for your bakery, "Sweet Delights." Here's how you might configure the basic settings:

1. **Site Title**: "Sweet Delights Bakery"
2. **Tagline**: "Delicious Cakes, Made Fresh Every Day"
3. **Permalinks**: Set to "Post name" for clean, SEO-friendly URLs.
4. **Timezone**: Set to your local timezone, e.g., "New York" if your bakery is in New York.
5. **Comment Settings**: You may decide to approve comments manually for a more controlled approach to user interaction.
6. **Discussion**: Enable comment notifications, so you're aware of new interactions on your site.

Once these settings are configured, your site will be personalized and properly set up to reflect your business's unique identity.

You'll be ready to dive deeper into customizing your website further in the next chapters.

This chapter provides a comprehensive introduction to navigating the WordPress Dashboard and managing essential settings. In the next chapter, we'll explore how to enhance your site's appearance by choosing and customizing WordPress themes.

Chapter 4: Themes and Theme Customization

WordPress themes are the backbone of your website's design and layout. They control the visual aesthetics, structure, and presentation of your content. This chapter will introduce you to the concept of WordPress themes, guide you in choosing the right theme for your project, and show you how to customize a theme to fit your needs, using the example of customizing the "Twenty Twenty-Three" theme for a blog site.

What are Themes?: Understanding WordPress Themes and How They Shape a Site's Design

A **WordPress theme** is a collection of files that work together to define the layout and design of a WordPress website. These files include templates for individual pages, CSS styles for styling the content, and JavaScript for interactive elements. Think of a theme as the "skin" of your website — it determines the look and feel, but not the content itself.

Key Components of a WordPress Theme:

1. **Templates**: Templates are the backbone of how your pages are structured. For instance, the "single.php" template might define the layout of a blog post, while "page.php"

could define how static pages like "About" or "Contact" are displayed.

2. **Stylesheets**: These control the visual design elements, such as fonts, colors, spacing, and layout.

3. **JavaScript**: Adds interactive features like sliders, modal windows, or pop-up notifications.

4. **Functions.php**: A special file that allows you to add custom functions and features to your theme without modifying the core files.

Themes can be either free or premium. Free themes are available from the WordPress repository, while premium themes are sold by third-party vendors and often come with more advanced features, customization options, and support.

Choosing the Right Theme: How to Select a Theme that Fits Your Project

Choosing the right theme for your project is a crucial step in building a WordPress website. The theme should not only be visually appealing but also support the functionality you need for your website.

Here are a few factors to consider when selecting a theme:

1. **Purpose of the Site**

o Consider the type of site you are building (blog, business site, eCommerce, portfolio, etc.) and look for a theme that aligns with the purpose. For instance, a business site may require a theme that supports contact forms, testimonials, and service listings, while a blog theme will focus on readability and post layout.

2. **Responsive Design**

o A responsive theme automatically adjusts to look good on all devices — desktops, tablets, and smartphones. This is essential, as a large portion of website traffic comes from mobile devices.

3. **Customization Options**

o Some themes come with built-in customization options through the WordPress Customizer, such as logo upload, color changes, font selection, and layout controls. If you want full control over the design, opt for a theme that offers extensive customization without the need for code.

4. **SEO-Friendly**

o SEO-friendly themes are optimized for search engines, making it easier for your site to rank well on Google. Look for themes that are clean, fast-loading, and follow the best SEO practices (like proper heading structure and mobile optimization).

5. **Theme Support and Updates**

   o Choose a theme that's regularly updated and has good customer support. Premium themes, in particular, often offer access to dedicated support teams and more frequent updates to keep up with the latest WordPress changes.

6. **Performance**

   o A theme with a lot of features or heavy design elements can slow down your site. Choose a theme that's optimized for speed and performance, as a slow-loading site can hurt your user experience and SEO rankings.

7. **Theme Compatibility with Plugins**

   o Ensure that the theme is compatible with essential plugins (like WooCommerce for eCommerce, Yoast SEO for optimization, or Contact Form 7 for forms). This ensures your site's functionality is not compromised.

Real-World Example: Customizing the "Twenty Twenty-Three" Theme for a Blog Site

To demonstrate theme customization, let's work with the default WordPress theme, **Twenty Twenty-Three**. This theme is a good starting point for a blog site because of its clean design and flexibility.

Here's how to customize the **Twenty Twenty-Three** theme for a blog site:

1. **Activate the Theme**
   - First, make sure the "Twenty Twenty-Three" theme is installed and activated. You can do this by navigating to **Appearance** → **Themes** in the WordPress Dashboard and selecting **Activate** under the "Twenty Twenty-Three" theme.

2. **Customizing the Site Identity**
   - Go to **Appearance** → **Customize** to open the WordPress Customizer. From here, click on **Site Identity**.
   - **Site Title**: Enter your blog's name, such as "Tech Tips Blog."
   - **Tagline**: Add a catchy description, e.g., "Your daily source of tech advice."
   - **Site Icon**: Upload a small image that will appear in browser tabs and bookmarks.

3. **Selecting a Header Image**
   - In the Customizer, click on **Header Media** to add a header image to your blog. Choose an image that represents the theme of your blog. For example, a

tech blog might use an image of a laptop or coding interface.

- o If you don't want a header image, you can remove it and opt for a clean design that focuses on the typography.

4. **Changing Colors and Fonts**

- o Under the **Colors** section in the Customizer, you can adjust the site's primary color. You might want to choose a color that matches your brand or gives your blog a professional look.

- o Go to the **Typography** section to change the font family, size, and style for the body and headings. For a blog, you'll want a legible font for reading long posts, like "Roboto" or "Open Sans."

5. **Menu Configuration**

- o To set up a navigation menu, go to **Appearance** → **Menus** and create a new menu. You can add links to important pages like "About," "Contact," and "Blog."

- o You can also organize categories as menu items so that visitors can easily navigate your blog's topics.

6. **Widgets for Sidebar and Footer**

- o WordPress allows you to add widgets to your site's sidebar or footer. You can add recent posts, search bars, categories, and more to help users easily navigate your blog.

- ○ Go to **Appearance** → **Widgets** to add widgets to areas like the Sidebar or Footer.

7. **Creating Blog Posts and Categories**
   - ○ Now that your theme is set up, start adding content. Go to **Posts** → **Add New** to create a blog post.
   - ○ Organize your posts into categories (e.g., "Tech News," "How-Tos," "Reviews") to make it easier for readers to find content that interests them.

8. **Responsive Design Check**
   - ○ Once your theme is customized, check how it looks on different devices by using the device preview options in the Customizer. Ensure the layout adjusts properly for mobile phones and tablets.

By following these steps, you can create a simple yet functional blog site using the "Twenty Twenty-Three" theme. However, if you want to further personalize the design, you can dive into custom CSS or even child theme development (covered in later chapters).

WordPress themes are essential for shaping the design and layout of your website. In this chapter, we've learned how to navigate the

WordPress theme system, select the right theme for your project, and customize the "Twenty Twenty-Three" theme for a blog site. With a solid understanding of themes, you can start building websites that look and perform well, all without writing any code.

In the next chapter, we'll explore the world of **WordPress Plugins**, which enhance your site's functionality and allow you to add custom features easily.

Chapter 5: Installing and Configuring Plugins

Plugins are what give WordPress its incredible flexibility and scalability. While WordPress comes with a variety of built-in features, plugins allow you to extend those features, add new functionalities, and easily customize your site. In this chapter, we'll dive into the world of WordPress plugins, show you how to install and configure them, and provide real-world examples to help you get started with essential plugins.

What are Plugins?: How Plugins Add Functionality to WordPress Sites

A **plugin** is a piece of software that integrates with WordPress to add specific features or functions. WordPress plugins are essentially extensions that can make your site more dynamic by providing additional functionality such as SEO optimization, contact forms, social sharing, backups, and much more.

- **Customization**: Plugins allow you to customize your site without needing to touch the core WordPress code.
- **Pre-built Solutions**: Rather than building a feature from scratch, plugins offer pre-built solutions to common needs, making WordPress development faster and more efficient.

- **Plugin Ecosystem**: The WordPress Plugin Directory hosts over 50,000 plugins, many of which are free. There are also premium plugins available from third-party developers for more advanced functionalities.

Key Types of Plugins:

- **SEO Plugins**: Enhance your site's SEO to help it rank better in search engines (e.g., Yoast SEO).
- **Security Plugins**: Protect your website from malware, brute-force attacks, and other vulnerabilities (e.g., Wordfence).
- **Contact Form Plugins**: Add customizable forms to your site (e.g., Contact Form 7).
- **E-commerce Plugins**: Add e-commerce functionality to turn your WordPress site into an online store (e.g., WooCommerce).
- **Backup Plugins**: Automate the process of backing up your site (e.g., UpdraftPlus).

Plugins give you the freedom to focus on content and user experience while adding complex functionality without the need for coding.

Top Plugins for Beginners: Installing and Configuring Essential Plugins

Here are a few essential plugins that can significantly enhance your WordPress site. These plugins are ideal for beginners and will help you improve site performance, security, and usability:

1. **Yoast SEO** (Search Engine Optimization)
   - **Purpose**: Helps you optimize your site for search engines by providing on-page SEO analysis, keyword optimization, and XML sitemaps.
   - **Installation**: To install Yoast SEO, go to **Plugins → Add New**, search for "Yoast SEO," and click **Install Now**. Once installed, click **Activate**.
   - **Configuration**: After activation, go to the new **SEO** menu in your dashboard. Follow the configuration wizard to set up site titles, meta descriptions, and other SEO basics.

2. **Contact Form 7** (Contact Forms)
   - **Purpose**: Easily add a contact form to your site. Visitors can fill in their details, and you'll receive the messages via email.
   - **Installation**: Go to **Plugins → Add New**, search for "Contact Form 7," then click **Install Now** and **Activate**.
   - **Configuration**: After activation, you'll find **Contact** in your dashboard menu. Create a new

form and copy the shortcode provided. Paste this shortcode into any post or page to display the form.

3. **UpdraftPlus** (Backup Plugin)

   o **Purpose**: Automatically back up your website files and database, providing peace of mind in case anything goes wrong.

   o **Installation**: Go to **Plugins** → **Add New**, search for "UpdraftPlus," then click **Install Now** and **Activate**.

   o **Configuration**: Go to **Settings** → **UpdraftPlus Backups**. From here, you can schedule automatic backups and select remote storage options (e.g., Google Drive or Dropbox).

4. **Wordfence Security** (Security Plugin)

   o **Purpose**: Protect your WordPress site from malicious attacks, hackers, and spam.

   o **Installation**: Go to **Plugins** → **Add New**, search for "Wordfence," then click **Install Now** and **Activate**.

   o **Configuration**: After activation, the plugin will guide you through a basic setup. You can adjust security settings like firewall protection, login attempt limits, and email alerts for suspicious activities.

5. **WooCommerce** (E-commerce Plugin)

- o **Purpose**: Turn your WordPress site into a fully functional online store.

- o **Installation**: Go to **Plugins** → **Add New**, search for "WooCommerce," then click **Install Now** and **Activate**.

- o **Configuration**: WooCommerce includes a setup wizard to guide you through store setup, including payment gateways, shipping options, and tax configurations.

Real-World Example: Adding a Contact Form and SEO Plugin to Your Site

Let's walk through adding two essential plugins — **Contact Form 7** and **Yoast SEO** — to a simple WordPress blog. These plugins are commonly used by site owners to enhance user interaction and optimize content for search engines.

---

1. Adding a Contact Form Using Contact Form 7

A contact form allows visitors to get in touch with you directly from your website. Here's how to set one up using **Contact Form 7**:

1. **Install and Activate**:

o Go to **Plugins** → **Add New**, search for "Contact Form 7," and click **Install Now**. Once installed, click **Activate**.

2. **Create a Contact Form**:

  o After activation, you'll see a **Contact** menu in the dashboard. Click on **Contact** → **Add New** to create a new form.

  o The default form will include fields like Name, Email, and Message. You can customize these fields if you need additional options (e.g., phone number or subject).

3. **Configure the Form**:

  o In the form editor, you can modify the email address that receives the form submissions by editing the "Mail" tab.

  o The **Mail** section allows you to set the "To" email address, which is where messages will be sent.

4. **Insert the Form into a Page**:

  o After saving the form, you will get a shortcode (e.g., [contact-form-7 id="1234" title="Contact form 1"]).

  o Copy this shortcode and paste it into any page or post where you want the form to appear (e.g., the "Contact Us" page).

2. Optimizing Your Content Using Yoast SEO

To make sure your WordPress site is optimized for search engines, **Yoast SEO** is a powerful tool to guide you through proper SEO practices:

1. **Install and Activate**:
   - Go to **Plugins** → **Add New**, search for "Yoast SEO," then click **Install Now** and **Activate**.
2. **Configure Basic Settings**:
   - After activation, you'll find a new **SEO** menu in the dashboard. Click on **SEO** → **General**.
   - Use the configuration wizard to set up your site. Enter your site's name, logo, and social media profiles. This information will be used to generate SEO-friendly meta data.
3. **SEO Optimization for a Post**:
   - Go to any post or page, and scroll down to find the **Yoast SEO** section.
   - Enter a **Focus Keyphrase** (the main keyword you want to rank for). Yoast will then provide recommendations for optimizing your content, such as adding the keyphrase to headings, body text, and meta description.
   - Yoast will give you a **SEO score** and a **readability score** to guide improvements.
4. **XML Sitemaps**:

o   Yoast automatically generates an XML sitemap for your site, which helps search engines index your content more efficiently. You can find the sitemap URL under **SEO → General → Features**.

Plugins are essential tools that extend the functionality of your WordPress site. In this chapter, we've covered the basics of plugins, how they add valuable features to your site, and provided a step-by-step guide to installing and configuring essential plugins.

In the next chapter, we'll explore **Content Management in WordPress**, focusing on creating posts, pages, and managing media to help you build rich, engaging content for your website.

Chapter 6: Creating Content with WordPress

Content is at the heart of any WordPress website. Whether you're running a blog, a business site, or an e-commerce platform, creating and managing content is essential for engaging your audience and conveying your message. In this chapter, we'll dive into the various ways to create content using WordPress, explore the differences between posts and pages, and learn how to use the WordPress Block Editor (Gutenberg) to build visually rich, dynamic pages and posts.

Posts vs Pages: Understanding the Difference and When to Use Each

One of the first decisions you'll make when creating content in WordPress is whether to create a **post** or a **page**. While both are used to display content on your website, they serve different purposes.

1. **Posts**:
    - **Purpose**: Posts are used for regularly updated content such as blog articles, news, or other types of dynamic content. Posts are typically displayed in

WordPress Development Guide
WordPress Development Guide

reverse chronological order on the homepage or blog page.

- o **Characteristics**:
  - ▪ **Date-Driven**: Posts are usually time-sensitive and organized by date.
  - ▪ **Categories and Tags**: Posts can be categorized into different topics and tagged with keywords, making it easier for users to find related content.
  - ▪ **Social Media and RSS**: Posts are often shared on social media or syndicated via RSS feeds.

When to Use Posts:

- o Use posts when you have content that will be updated regularly, such as blog articles, news updates, or product reviews.
- o Ideal for content that benefits from categorization and tagging, such as niche topics or thematic series.

2. **Pages**:
   - o **Purpose**: Pages are for static content that doesn't change frequently. Examples include an "About" page, "Contact Us," "Services," or "Privacy Policy."
   - o **Characteristics**:

- **No Time-Sensitivity**: Pages are not organized by date. They are typically displayed as part of your site's main structure (e.g., in your navigation menu).
- **Hierarchy**: Pages can have parent and child relationships, allowing you to create nested or hierarchical structures (e.g., "Contact Us" could have a child page "Contact Form").

When to Use Pages:

o Use pages for static content that doesn't change often and should be included in your website's navigation, such as your homepage, about us, and contact pages.

The Block Editor (Gutenberg): Creating and Managing Content Using Blocks

The **Block Editor** (also known as **Gutenberg**) is WordPress's modern content creation tool that allows you to build content using blocks. Each block represents a piece of content (e.g., text, image, video, quote) that can be easily manipulated and customized. This makes content creation more flexible, modular, and visually appealing.

1. **What is Gutenberg?**

   o Gutenberg is WordPress's default editor introduced in version 5.0, designed to offer a more intuitive and block-based approach to content creation. It replaces the classic editor with a more visual, user-friendly interface that allows you to arrange content in blocks.

   o Each block has its own settings and styling options, so you can create complex layouts without the need for coding or additional plugins.

2. **Types of Blocks**:

   o **Text Blocks**: Add text content with the **Paragraph** block. You can adjust fonts, alignments, and colors.

   o **Image Blocks**: Insert images directly into your posts or pages. Gutenberg also allows you to set image sizes, add captions, and adjust positioning.

   o **Heading Blocks**: Use different heading blocks to structure your content with clear headings and subheadings.

   o **List Blocks**: Easily add bulleted or numbered lists.

   o **Embed Blocks**: Embed media from external platforms like YouTube, Instagram, or Twitter.

   o **Button Blocks**: Add customizable call-to-action buttons to link to other pages or external sites.

    o **Custom HTML**: For advanced users, Gutenberg allows you to add custom HTML directly into your posts.

3. **Creating Content with Gutenberg**:

    o **Adding Blocks**: To add a block, click the + button located at the top-left corner of the editor. You can search for a specific block or browse through the available categories.

    o **Arranging Blocks**: You can rearrange blocks by dragging and dropping them. This makes it easy to reorder your content as needed.

    o **Customizing Blocks**: Once you add a block, you can customize it by adjusting settings in the block toolbar and the block settings panel that appears on the right-hand side of the editor.

    o **Reusable Blocks**: If you create a block you want to use across multiple posts or pages, you can save it as a **Reusable Block**. This is ideal for elements like call-to-action buttons, contact forms, or specific layouts.

4. **Preview and Publish**:

    o Once your content is ready, you can preview it to see how it will look to your audience. After making any necessary tweaks, hit **Publish** to make the content live on your website.

Real-World Example: Building a Blog Post and a Landing Page

To give you a practical understanding of how to create content with WordPress, let's walk through two real-world examples: creating a blog post and a landing page.

1. Building a Blog Post

Let's create a blog post about "Top 5 SEO Tips for Beginners."

Step 1: Create a New Post

- From the WordPress Dashboard, go to **Posts** → **Add New**.
- In the editor, give your post a title, for example, "Top 5 SEO Tips for Beginners."

Step 2: Add Content Blocks

- Start with a **Heading** block to introduce the topic: "SEO Tip #1: Keyword Research."
- Below it, add a **Paragraph** block to explain the first tip in detail.
- Continue by adding other **Heading** blocks for each tip, followed by a **Paragraph** block for detailed descriptions.
- Insert an **Image** block if you have relevant images (e.g., a screenshot of Google Keyword Planner).

- At the end, use a **Button** block to create a call-to-action (e.g., "Learn More About SEO" linking to an external resource or a related page).

Step 3: Formatting and SEO

- Use the **Paragraph** block to add text content and style it (bold, italics, links).
- Don't forget to use Yoast SEO (installed plugin) to set up the focus keyword, meta description, and SEO title.
- Once satisfied, hit **Publish**.

---

2. Creating a Landing Page

Now, let's create a **Landing Page** for a new service you're offering.

Step 1: Create a New Page

- From the Dashboard, go to **Pages → Add New**.
- Give your page a title, such as "Our New SEO Service."

Step 2: Add a Hero Section

- Start by adding a **Group Block** (which allows you to combine multiple blocks).

- Inside the group, add an **Image** block for a hero image and a **Heading** block for the title of the service.
- Follow this with a **Paragraph** block describing the service and its benefits.

Step 3: Add Call-to-Action

- After the main content, add a **Button** block that says "Get Started" or "Contact Us."
- Set the button link to the appropriate page (e.g., a contact form or booking page).

Step 4: Customize for Layout

- Adjust the layout and spacing by using blocks like **Spacer** or **Separator** to make the page visually appealing and easy to read.

Step 5: Preview and Publish

- Once satisfied with the layout and content, preview the page to ensure everything looks great.
- Hit **Publish** to make your landing page live.

Creating content in WordPress is a straightforward and powerful process, thanks to the flexibility of the Block Editor (Gutenberg). Whether you are publishing regular blog posts or building static landing pages, WordPress gives you all the tools you need to create engaging, well-structured content. In this chapter, we've explored the differences between posts and pages, the features of the Block Editor, and walked through real-world examples for both a blog post and a landing page.

In the next chapter, we'll dive into **WordPress Media Management**, exploring how to upload, organize, and optimize images and other media for a better user experience.

Chapter 7: Customizing Your Site with Widgets and Menus

WordPress allows you to customize your site's layout and functionality in a variety of ways, and two of the most important tools for doing so are **widgets** and **menus**. Widgets allow you to add extra functionality to areas like sidebars, footers, and other widget-ready sections of your site. Menus, on the other hand, help you create clear navigation structures, making it easier for visitors to explore your website. In this chapter, we will explore both widgets and menus in-depth, and demonstrate how you can use them to enhance your site.

Widgets: Adding Functionality to Your Site's Sidebar and Footer
What Are Widgets?

Widgets are small blocks of content or functionality that can be added to specific areas of your WordPress site, such as the sidebar, footer, or other widget-ready sections. Widgets can display anything from recent blog posts, social media feeds, or search bars, to custom HTML, and even videos. They allow you to easily add extra functionality to your site without needing to write any code.

1. **Accessing and Adding Widgets**:

- To access the widget area, go to your WordPress Dashboard, then navigate to **Appearance** → **Widgets**.
- On this page, you will see a list of available widgets on the left and a preview of widget-ready areas (such as sidebars and footers) on the right.

2. **Popular Widgets You Can Add**:
   - **Recent Posts**: Displays a list of the latest posts published on your site.
   - **Search**: Adds a search bar to your sidebar or footer, allowing users to search for content on your site.
   - **Text**: Displays custom text or HTML, which is useful for adding a message, banner, or a small call-to-action.
   - **Custom HTML**: You can add your own custom HTML code here, such as embedding a YouTube video, a form, or custom scripts.
   - **Social Media Feeds**: Displays social media links or feeds directly on your website (usually through a plugin).

3. **Drag and Drop Widgets**:
   - To add a widget, simply drag it from the left panel to a widget-ready area on the right, like the **Sidebar** or **Footer**.

o Each widget has its own settings, allowing you to customize things like the number of posts to display, titles, or other configuration options.

4. **Removing or Reordering Widgets**:

o To remove a widget, drag it back to the left side or click on the **Remove** link in the widget's settings.

o To reorder widgets, drag them to different positions within a widget area.

Menus: Creating Navigation Menus to Structure Your Site

What Are Menus?

Menus are essential for structuring your site's navigation, helping visitors find their way around your site. WordPress allows you to create custom menus for different parts of your website, such as the main navigation bar, footer menu, or even custom menus for specific pages.

1. **Creating a Menu**:

o To create a new menu, go to **Appearance** → **Menus** in your WordPress dashboard.

o Here, you can create a new menu, give it a name, and start adding items to it. You can add **Pages**, **Posts**, **Custom Links**, and even **Categories** to your menu.

2. **Menu Locations**:

  ○ WordPress themes typically define specific locations where menus can be displayed. Common locations include:

    ▪ **Primary Menu** (usually at the top of the page)

    ▪ **Footer Menu** (usually at the bottom)

    ▪ **Mobile Menu** (on mobile versions of your site)

  ○ To assign your new menu to a location, check the appropriate box under **Menu Settings** and save your changes.

3. **Adding Menu Items**:

  ○ Once your menu is created, you can add items. For example:

    ▪ **Pages**: Select from your existing pages like the homepage, about page, or contact page.

    ▪ **Posts**: If you want to link to a specific blog post, you can add it to the menu.

    ▪ **Custom Links**: You can add external URLs, like social media profiles or an affiliate link.

    ▪ **Categories**: Add categories to the menu, so users can browse all posts within a particular category.

4. **Menu Structure and Submenus**:

- o You can easily create submenus (drop-down menus) by dragging and dropping items slightly to the right underneath a parent item.
- o This is helpful for structuring your navigation logically, for example, grouping blog categories or services under main menu headings.

5. **Customizing Menu Appearance**:
   - o Most WordPress themes allow you to customize the appearance of your menus (e.g., changing font sizes, colors, hover effects). Some of these options can be adjusted through the WordPress customizer (**Appearance → Customize → Menus**), or by adding custom CSS to your theme.

Real-World Example: Adding a Social Media Widget and a Navigation Menu

Let's walk through a practical example of adding both a social media widget and a navigation menu to your site.

Example 1: Adding a Social Media Widget

Step 1: Go to **Appearance → Widgets** in your WordPress Dashboard. **Step 2**: In the **Available Widgets** panel, search for a widget called "Social Media" or "Social Icons" (This might be a plugin or theme feature, or you may need to install a plugin such as "Simple Social Icons"). **Step 3**: Drag the widget to the **Sidebar** or **Footer** area, depending on where you want the icons to appear. **Step 4**: Configure the widget by adding your social media URLs (e.g., Facebook, Twitter, Instagram). **Step 5**: Save the widget, and the social media icons will now appear on your site.

Example 2: Creating a Navigation Menu

Step 1: Go to **Appearance** → **Menus** in your WordPress Dashboard. **Step 2**: Click **Create a New Menu**, give it a name (e.g., "Main Navigation"), and click **Create Menu**. **Step 3**: Add pages to the menu by selecting them from the left column and clicking **Add to Menu**.

- Example: Add the "Home," "About Us," and "Services" pages to the menu. **Step 4**: For a submenu, drag a page or link slightly to the right beneath a parent item (e.g., dragging "Blog" under "Services"). **Step 5**: Assign the menu to the **Primary Menu** location and save it.

Now your site will have a structured, easy-to-navigate menu and a functional social media widget, allowing visitors to navigate through your content and connect with your social media profiles.

In this chapter, we've learned how to customize your WordPress site by adding and configuring widgets and menus. Widgets are essential for adding dynamic functionality like social media links, recent posts, or search bars to your site's sidebar or footer. Menus, on the other hand, help structure your site's navigation, ensuring that visitors can easily find and access the content they're looking for.

By using these tools, you can improve your site's usability and make it more interactive, while ensuring that visitors have a seamless experience on both desktop and mobile devices. In the next chapter, we'll dive into **WordPress Security**, learning how to protect your site from common security threats and vulnerabilities.

Chapter 8: Managing Media Files in WordPress

WordPress makes it easy to manage media files—images, audio, video, and documents—across your site. However, to maintain a fast and user-friendly site, it's crucial to not only upload your media files correctly but also to optimize them for performance. In this chapter, we will dive into how to efficiently manage media files in WordPress, optimize images for faster loading times, and walk through a real-world example of adding and optimizing images for a photo gallery.

Uploading Media: Images, Audio, Video, and Documents
How to Upload Media in WordPress:

WordPress allows you to easily upload various types of media to your website through the **Media Library**. The types of media you can upload include:

1. **Images** (e.g., JPEG, PNG, GIF, WebP)
2. **Audio files** (e.g., MP3, WAV, OGG)
3. **Video files** (e.g., MP4, MOV, AVI)
4. **Documents** (e.g., PDF, DOCX, PPTX, CSV)

Step-by-Step Media Upload:

1. **Via the Dashboard:**
   - Navigate to **Media → Add New** in your WordPress dashboard.
   - Click **Select Files**, and a dialog will open, allowing you to choose the media files from your computer.
   - You can upload multiple files at once by selecting them all together.

2. **From the Block Editor:**
   - When creating or editing a post or page, simply click on the + button to add a block and select the **Image**, **Video**, or **Audio** block.
   - Click on **Upload** or select **Media Library** to add existing files from your library.

3. **Via Drag-and-Drop:**
   - You can also drag and drop media files directly into the Media Library, which will automatically upload the files to your site.

Image Optimization: Tools and Techniques to Optimize Media for Performance

Images are typically the largest media files on websites and can significantly impact site speed. Optimizing images is one of the most effective ways to improve your website's loading time. Here are key techniques and tools for image optimization:

1. Choose the Right Image Format:

- **JPEG**: Ideal for photographs and images with lots of colors. It has a good balance between quality and file size.
- **PNG**: Best for images that require transparency or images with sharp edges (like logos). However, PNG files tend to be larger than JPEGs.
- **WebP**: A newer image format that provides high-quality images with smaller file sizes. It's supported by most modern browsers.

2. Resize Images:

- Avoid uploading images that are larger than they need to be. Resize images to fit the dimensions that will be used on your site (e.g., resizing a hero image to the width of your website's header).
- WordPress automatically generates several sizes of each image you upload, including thumbnail, medium, and large sizes. You can manage these sizes in **Settings → Media** in your dashboard.

3. Compress Images:

- Use image compression to reduce file sizes without sacrificing too much quality. You can use tools like:

o **TinyPNG**: An online tool that reduces image size while maintaining quality.

o **ImageOptim**: A desktop app for compressing images.

o **ShortPixel**: A WordPress plugin that compresses images automatically on upload.

4. Lazy Loading:

- Enable **lazy loading** for images. This means that images only load when they are about to be visible on the user's screen, which reduces initial page load times.

- WordPress 5.5+ comes with lazy loading enabled by default, but you can customize or disable it if necessary using plugins or custom code.

5. Use a Content Delivery Network (CDN):

- A CDN stores copies of your images (and other media files) on servers around the world, allowing users to download them from a server closest to their location, improving load times.

Real-World Example: Adding and Optimizing Images for a Photo Gallery

Now that we've covered how to upload and optimize media in WordPress, let's walk through a real-world example of creating a **photo gallery**. We'll go through the process of uploading images, optimizing them for performance, and displaying them beautifully on your site.

Step 1: Uploading Images for the Gallery

1. Navigate to your **Dashboard** and go to **Media → Add New**.
2. Click **Select Files** and choose the images you want to upload for the gallery. Select several images from your computer or drag and drop them directly into the Media Library.
3. After the images are uploaded, you can click on each image in the Media Library to edit their details, such as the **Alt Text**, **Title**, **Caption**, and **Description**. These details help with SEO and accessibility.

Step 2: Optimizing the Images

1. Use a tool like **TinyPNG** or **ShortPixel** to compress the images before uploading them. If you're uploading large images, it's especially important to reduce their file sizes to improve load times.
2. Resize the images to match the maximum size used on your site. For example, if your photo gallery will display images

at 800px wide, resize the images accordingly before uploading them.

3. If you're using WebP images, consider converting them from other formats to reduce file size even further.

Step 3: Creating the Gallery

1. In your WordPress post or page editor, click on the + button to add a block and choose the **Gallery** block.

2. Select **Create a New Gallery**, and then choose the images you uploaded in the previous step.

3. You can reorder the images by dragging them or remove any unwanted images by clicking the **Delete** icon.

4. Once you've selected your images, click **Insert Gallery**.

Step 4: Customizing the Gallery Layout

1. The default gallery block in WordPress displays images in a grid. You can customize the number of columns by adjusting the **Columns** setting in the block editor.

2. If you want a more advanced gallery layout, consider using a plugin like **Envira Gallery** or **NextGEN Gallery**, which offer additional customization options such as lightboxes, slideshows, and more.

Step 5: Preview and Publish

Once your gallery is set up, preview your page to make sure everything looks good. Ensure that the images are loading quickly, the layout looks nice, and the gallery is responsive (i.e., it adapts to different screen sizes, including mobile devices). When you're satisfied, hit **Publish** or **Update** to make your gallery live.

In this chapter, we covered how to efficiently manage media files in WordPress by uploading, optimizing, and displaying them. We learned the importance of choosing the right image format, resizing and compressing images, enabling lazy loading, and using a CDN to enhance performance. Additionally, we walked through a real-world example of adding and optimizing images for a photo gallery, which is a common feature for many WordPress sites.

By properly managing your media and optimizing images, you can significantly improve your site's loading speed, SEO, and user experience. In the next chapter, we will explore **WordPress SEO**, where we'll discuss how to make your site more visible to search engines and attract more visitors.

Chapter 9: WordPress Users and Permissions

WordPress allows you to build and manage websites with a strong focus on user management. Whether you're running a personal blog or a large eCommerce site, the ability to control who can access certain parts of your website and what actions they can take is essential. This is where **user roles** and **permissions** come into play. In this chapter, we'll explore how to manage user roles, set appropriate permissions, and create a **multi-author blog** with custom roles.

Managing User Roles: Admin, Editor, Author, Contributor, and Subscriber

WordPress provides a flexible system for managing user roles and assigning different capabilities to each user. These roles define what users can and cannot do within your site's dashboard. By understanding and assigning the correct roles, you ensure that each user has the appropriate level of access based on their responsibilities.

Here's an overview of the five default user roles in WordPress:

1. **Administrator (Admin):**

- o **Capabilities**: Administrators have the highest level of access to the WordPress dashboard. They can perform all actions, including managing themes and plugins, adding users, editing content, and changing site settings.
- o **When to Use**: The Administrator role should be reserved for trusted individuals who need full access to the site, such as website owners and developers.

2. **Editor:**

- o **Capabilities**: Editors can manage and publish content, including posts and pages. They can edit, publish, and delete any content created by any user, but they cannot manage site settings, themes, or plugins.
- o **When to Use**: Editors are typically used for managing editorial teams. They're ideal for people responsible for overseeing and editing content without needing full access to site settings.

3. **Author:**

- o **Capabilities**: Authors can write, edit, publish, and delete their own posts. They cannot modify or manage the content of other users.
- o **When to Use**: The Author role is perfect for individual content creators who will be contributing

their own posts but do not need access to other site content or settings.

4. **Contributor:**

   o **Capabilities**: Contributors can write and manage their own posts but cannot publish them. They also cannot upload files, such as images, but can submit posts for review by an Editor or Administrator.

   o **When to Use**: This role is typically used for guest writers or collaborators who need to contribute content but don't have permission to publish it themselves.

5. **Subscriber:**

   o **Capabilities**: Subscribers can only manage their user profiles, including changing their password and email address. They cannot write posts or access the WordPress dashboard.

   o **When to Use**: Subscribers are ideal for users who simply need to interact with the content on your site, such as reading posts or commenting, but don't require any administrative capabilities.

Setting Permissions: Controlling What Each User Can Access and Modify

WordPress's user role system comes with predefined permissions, but it's also highly flexible, allowing you to control exactly what each user can and cannot do. Permissions can be controlled on two levels:

1. **Role-Based Permissions:** As we discussed, each user role comes with a set of permissions. These permissions are predefined, but you can modify them using plugins or custom code if you need more control.

2. **Content-Based Permissions:** WordPress allows you to set permissions for specific types of content. For instance, you can restrict access to certain posts or pages based on the user role. You can also control who can see certain posts or content using plugins like **User Access Manager** or **Restrict Content Pro**.

Some actions, like publishing posts or moderating comments, can be controlled at the content level, meaning that only users with the necessary role (Editor, Author, etc.) will be able to access those features. This is useful if you want to limit access to certain pieces of content based on user responsibility.

Plugins for Advanced Permission Management:

- **Members**: A popular plugin that allows you to create and manage custom roles and capabilities. This plugin can be particularly useful for more complex permission systems.

- **User Role Editor**: A plugin that allows you to manage, edit, and create custom roles with specific permissions for your WordPress site.

Real-World Example: Creating a Multi-Author Blog with Custom Roles

In this example, we'll create a multi-author blog where several contributors can write posts, but only specific users (such as Editors and Admins) can publish them.

Step 1: Create the Contributors' Roles

1. **Install the User Role Editor Plugin** (if needed) to modify user roles and capabilities.
2. Go to **Users → User Role Editor** and create a new role called **Contributor Plus** (or any custom name).
3. For this new role, grant the ability to write and edit posts but not publish. You can also allow file uploads for images or videos that contributors can use in their posts.
4. Assign this role to all writers who will contribute to the blog but should not have the ability to publish content directly.

Step 2: Create the Editors' Roles

1. Editors should have the permission to publish content. However, you may want to further customize their permissions.

2. Go to **Users** → **All Users**, and ensure that the Editors have access to posts written by others. You may also grant them permission to moderate comments and view site statistics.

Step 3: Assign Roles to Users

1. Go to **Users** → **All Users**, and assign the appropriate role to each user. Assign **Contributor Plus** to the writers and **Editor** to the individuals who will oversee the published content.

2. You can also assign **Admin** roles to the individuals who will have full access to the site and manage the users.

Step 4: Content Workflow and Review Process

1. Contributors can now submit posts, but only Editors can review, edit, and publish them.

2. Set up an editorial workflow where Editors can assign tasks to Contributors or approve content after reviewing.

3. You can add additional steps, like having an Administrator review posts from Editors before they're published.

Step 5: Publishing the Content When a post is ready for publishing, an Editor can simply click the **Publish** button. If the

Editor is unsure about the post's final version, they can leave it in **Draft** mode, allowing for revisions.

In this chapter, we've explored the different user roles and permissions available in WordPress. By understanding the **Administrator**, **Editor**, **Author**, **Contributor**, and **Subscriber** roles, you can ensure that your site's users have the appropriate level of access. We also discussed how to fine-tune permissions and use plugins to create custom roles for more advanced access control.

A multi-author blog with custom roles allows for a streamlined editorial workflow where contributors write content, but only certain users have the authority to publish it. This workflow ensures that content is reviewed and approved before it goes live.

In the next chapter, we'll explore **WordPress SEO**, focusing on techniques and plugins to optimize your site for search engines and attract more visitors.

Chapter 10: Building a Contact Form

A **contact form** is an essential element for most websites, allowing visitors to reach out for inquiries, feedback, or support. Whether you're running a blog, eCommerce site, or a business website, having an easy-to-use, customizable contact form can improve communication with your audience. WordPress offers a range of powerful plugins that make creating and managing contact forms a breeze, as well as customization options for more specific needs. In this chapter, we'll walk through the process of building a contact form using popular WordPress plugins, how to customize the form fields, and a real-world example of creating a customer support form for a business website.

Using Contact Form Plugins: Best Practices and Tools like WPForms or Contact Form 7

While it's possible to manually code contact forms in WordPress, using a plugin saves time and ensures reliability and ease of use. There are several **contact form plugins** available in the WordPress Plugin Repository, but two of the most popular are **WPForms** and **Contact Form 7**.

WPForms:

WPForms is one of the easiest-to-use contact form plugins available. It comes with a drag-and-drop builder that makes creating forms a simple task, even for those without coding experience.

- **Features**:
  - Drag-and-drop form builder.
  - Pre-built form templates (Contact Form, Newsletter Signup, Payment Form, etc.).
  - Built-in spam protection (reCAPTCHA and Honeypot).
  - Email notifications and autoresponder.
  - Integration with payment platforms (PayPal, Stripe).
- **Best Practices**:
  - Keep forms simple: Ask for only the essential information to avoid overwhelming your visitors.
  - Use clear labels and instructions: Make sure visitors know what information is required.
  - Test the form: Always test your contact form to make sure submissions are working and notifications are sent.
  - Add reCAPTCHA or a spam filter to avoid spam submissions.

Contact Form 7:

Contact Form 7 is another widely used and free contact form plugin. Although it doesn't have the drag-and-drop functionality of

WPForms, it is flexible and can be customized with a little knowledge of HTML.

- **Features**:
  - Simple form creation using HTML.
  - Customizable email templates.
  - CAPTCHA and Akismet spam filtering.
  - Multi-form support (you can create multiple forms on the same website).
- **Best Practices**:
  - Keep it lightweight: Contact Form 7 can be extended with plugins, but it's best to avoid adding too many features to keep your form lean.
  - Customize your confirmation message: Once a user submits the form, customize the confirmation message so users know their inquiry has been received.
  - Configure email notifications: Ensure that the correct recipients get the form submission details.

Customizing Form Fields: Collecting the Right Information

When building a contact form, one of the most important things to consider is what kind of information you need to collect. Depending on the nature of your website (e.g., a business site, a blog, an eCommerce store), your contact form should be tailored to capture the necessary data without overwhelming the user.

Essential Form Fields:

Here are some common form fields you might include in your contact form:

1. **Name** (First and Last): To address the person properly.
2. **Email Address**: To ensure you can respond to the inquiry.
3. **Message**: A text box where users can type their questions or feedback.
4. **Phone Number** (optional): To provide additional support if needed.
5. **Subject**: To help categorize the inquiry (e.g., support, sales, feedback).
6. **Captcha/Spam Protection**: To avoid spam submissions.

Advanced Fields:

For more advanced use cases, you might want to collect more specific information or offer more personalized options. These could include:

1. **Dropdown Menus**: For users to select specific categories (e.g., "I need support with...").
2. **File Uploads**: For users to submit attachments (e.g., images or documents).

3. **Radio Buttons**: For users to select yes/no options or different types of requests.

4. **Date Picker**: For collecting dates, such as preferred appointment times.

Tips for Customization:

- **Conditional Logic**: WPForms allows you to create conditional fields, meaning that certain fields only appear based on a user's previous responses (e.g., if they select "Support" as the subject, a follow-up question asking for their order number could appear).

- **Customization through CSS**: For both WPForms and Contact Form 7, you can use custom CSS to tweak the form's look and feel, ensuring it matches your website's design.

Real-World Example: Creating a Customer Support Contact Form for a Business Website

Now that we've covered the basics of using contact form plugins and customizing fields, let's go through a practical example. Imagine you are building a customer support contact form for a business website that offers both product and service support. You want to capture relevant details to ensure you can assist customers effectively while making the form simple and user-friendly.

Step 1: Install and Activate WPForms

1. Go to your WordPress dashboard.
2. Navigate to **Plugins > Add New**.
3. Search for "WPForms" and click **Install Now**, then activate the plugin.

Step 2: Create a New Form

1. In the dashboard, go to **WPForms > Add New**.
2. Select the **Simple Contact Form** template, which will be the basis for your customer support form.
3. WPForms will automatically generate a basic form with the following fields: Name, Email, Message. You can customize these as needed.

Step 3: Add Custom Fields

- **Dropdown for Support Type**: Add a dropdown field to allow customers to specify the type of support they need (e.g., "Product Issue", "Account Issue", "Technical Support").
  - Drag the **Dropdown** field into the form.
  - Edit the options to match your categories.
- **File Upload**: If you want users to submit screenshots or other files related to their support request, add the **File Upload** field.

- o Drag the **File Upload** field into the form.
- o Set file size and types to allow only images or PDF files.
- **Phone Number**: If necessary, add a phone number field for customers who prefer to receive support over the phone.

Step 4: Customize the Form Settings

- **Email Notifications**: Go to **Settings > Notifications** and set up an email to be sent to the support team each time the form is submitted.
  - o You can customize the email subject and body, and even include form fields like the customer's name and the type of support needed.
- **Confirmation Message**: Go to **Settings > Confirmations** and create a custom message that will be displayed to the customer after they submit the form.
  - o Example: "Thank you for contacting us! Our support team will get back to you shortly."

Step 5: Embed the Form on Your Website

1. Go to the page or post where you want the form to appear.
2. In the WordPress editor, click on the + icon to add a block.
3. Search for **WPForms** and select the form you just created.
4. Publish or update the page.

Now, you've successfully created and embedded a customer support contact form. The form will capture all necessary details, such as the customer's issue type, message, and any files they want to upload, making it easier for your support team to assist them efficiently.

In this chapter, we learned how to create and manage contact forms in WordPress using plugins like **WPForms** and **Contact Form 7**. We discussed best practices for setting up forms, customizing the fields to collect the right information, and handling notifications. The real-world example of building a customer support form demonstrated how you can tailor forms to suit your business needs and streamline communication with your audience.

In the next chapter, we will dive into **WordPress SEO**, discussing how to optimize your website for search engines and attract more organic traffic.

Chapter 11: WordPress Security Best Practices

Security is a top priority for any website owner, and WordPress is no exception. Given its popularity, WordPress is often targeted by hackers and malicious actors. To safeguard your site and protect sensitive user data, it's important to implement solid security measures and regularly maintain your website. In this chapter, we will explore the basic security practices you should follow, tools that can help protect your site, and how to set up backups and restores. We'll also look at a real-world example of implementing SSL and installing a security plugin to help protect your WordPress website.

Securing WordPress: Basic Security Measures and Tools

When securing a WordPress site, there are several key areas you should focus on to mitigate the risk of unauthorized access and protect your data:

1. Keep WordPress, Themes, and Plugins Updated

- **Why Updates Matter**: WordPress frequently releases updates that fix bugs, patch security vulnerabilities, and improve performance. It's crucial to update both the WordPress core and any themes or plugins you're using.

Security exploits often arise from outdated software, so keeping everything up to date minimizes the risk.

- o **Action**: Set up automatic updates where possible, or regularly check for updates in the WordPress dashboard.

2. Strong Usernames and Passwords

- **Why Strong Passwords Matter**: Using weak or default passwords is one of the easiest ways for hackers to gain unauthorized access to your site. Passwords should be long, complex, and unique for each user.

  - o **Action**: Encourage users to create strong passwords with a combination of upper and lowercase letters, numbers, and special characters. Consider using a password manager to generate and store secure passwords.

3. Two-Factor Authentication (2FA)

- **Why 2FA Matters**: Two-factor authentication adds an extra layer of security by requiring users to provide a second form of authentication (e.g., a code sent to their phone) when logging in. This makes it significantly harder for hackers to compromise an account even if they have access to the password.

- o **Action**: Use plugins like **Google Authenticator** or **Wordfence Security** to enable 2FA for the admin login.

4. Limit Login Attempts

- **Why Limiting Attempts Matters**: Limiting the number of login attempts helps prevent brute-force attacks, where attackers try various username and password combinations until they find the correct one.
  - o **Action**: Install plugins like **Limit Login Attempts Reloaded** to restrict failed login attempts.

5. Secure Your wp-admin and wp-login.php

- **Why This is Important**: By default, the **wp-admin** dashboard and **wp-login.php** page are entry points for anyone trying to log into your WordPress site. Restricting access to these areas can prevent unauthorized access.
  - o **Action**: Consider using IP whitelisting or a security plugin to limit login attempts to specific IP addresses. You can also change the default login URL using plugins like **WPS Hide Login**.

6. Regularly Monitor User Activity

- **Why Monitoring Activity Matters**: By monitoring who logs into your site and what they do, you can spot any suspicious activity early and take action before a breach occurs.

  o **Action**: Use plugins like **WP Security Audit Log** to track user activities and monitor potential security risks.

Backup and Restore: Setting Up Regular Backups

Backups are critical to restoring your website if anything goes wrong—whether due to a security breach, server failure, or accidental data loss. A good backup strategy ensures that your website can be quickly restored to a previous state without losing valuable data.

1. Choosing a Backup Plugin

There are many backup plugins available that automate the backup process for WordPress. Two of the most reliable ones are **UpdraftPlus** and **BackWPup**.

- **UpdraftPlus**:
  o Backup files and databases to remote storage (e.g., Google Drive, Dropbox, Amazon S3).
  o Schedule automatic backups.
  o Restore with a single click.

- **BackWPup**:
  - Schedule backups and store them remotely (Dropbox, FTP, S3, etc.).
  - Offers both free and premium versions with advanced features.

2. How to Set Up Backups

- **Step 1**: Install and activate a backup plugin (e.g., UpdraftPlus).
- **Step 2**: Go to the plugin's settings page and choose where you want to store your backups (e.g., Google Drive, Dropbox).
- **Step 3**: Set up automatic backup schedules (daily, weekly, etc.) for your website files and database.
- **Step 4**: Test your backup by restoring your site to ensure it works properly.

3. Restoring Your Website

If your site is compromised or you experience data loss, you can restore it from a backup:

- **Step 1**: Install the backup plugin on your WordPress site.
- **Step 2**: Upload the backup file (from Google Drive, Dropbox, etc.).
- **Step 3**: Use the plugin's restore feature to revert your website to the backed-up version.

Having reliable backups means you can recover quickly from security incidents, ensuring minimal downtime and lost data.

Real-World Example: Implementing SSL and Installing a Security Plugin

One of the most important aspects of securing a WordPress site is ensuring that data transmitted between your users and your website is encrypted. This is where **SSL (Secure Socket Layer)** certificates come in. SSL secures the connection between the user's browser and the server, protecting sensitive data like login credentials and payment details.

1. Implementing SSL on Your WordPress Site

- **Why SSL Matters**: Google prioritizes sites with SSL encryption in search rankings, and many users expect their personal data to be encrypted when submitting forms or making purchases.
    - **Action**: To implement SSL:
        - **Step 1**: Purchase an SSL certificate from your hosting provider or use free services like **Let's Encrypt**.
        - **Step 2**: Install the SSL certificate on your web server (this process can vary depending on your hosting provider).

- **Step 3**: Update your WordPress site to use HTTPS instead of HTTP by changing the site URL in **Settings > General**.
- **Step 4**: Use a plugin like **Really Simple SSL** to automatically redirect visitors to the HTTPS version of your site.

2. Installing a Security Plugin

After implementing SSL, it's important to install a comprehensive security plugin to protect your site from threats like hacking attempts, malware, and brute-force attacks. A highly recommended plugin is **Wordfence Security**.

- **Why Wordfence Matters**: Wordfence offers both free and premium versions, providing features like:
  - Firewall protection to block malicious traffic.
  - Malware scanning to detect and remove threats.
  - Real-time security alerts and reports.

Steps to Install Wordfence:

- **Step 1**: Install Wordfence from the WordPress Plugin Repository.
- **Step 2**: Activate the plugin and go to **Wordfence > Dashboard** to start configuring the settings.
- **Step 3**: Enable the **Web Application Firewall** to block potential threats.

- **Step 4**: Set up **two-factor authentication (2FA)** to add an extra layer of protection to your login page.

In this chapter, we discussed the importance of securing your WordPress site and explored several key security measures, including keeping software up to date, using strong passwords, enabling two-factor authentication, limiting login attempts, and monitoring user activity. We also covered how to set up regular backups to protect your site's data and how to restore your website in case of an emergency.

Finally, we walked through a real-world example of implementing **SSL** to encrypt user data and installing a security plugin like **Wordfence** to strengthen your site's defenses.

With these security best practices in place, you'll be able to safeguard your WordPress site and ensure its integrity. In the next chapter, we will dive into **WordPress SEO**, helping you optimize your site for better visibility and higher rankings in search engine results.

Chapter 12: Optimizing WordPress for Speed

Website speed is critical to user experience and SEO. A slow-loading site can drive visitors away and negatively impact your search engine rankings. WordPress offers numerous tools and techniques to improve your site's performance, from caching to image optimization. In this chapter, we'll explore how to optimize your WordPress site for speed, including the use of caching plugins and image optimization. We'll also walk through a real-world example of speeding up a WordPress site using **WP Rocket** and image optimization tools.

Caching: Using Caching Plugins to Improve Performance

What is Caching?

Caching is the process of storing a version of your site's content in a temporary location so that it can be served to users more quickly. Instead of loading every element of your site each time a user visits, cached content delivers preloaded resources, significantly reducing load times.

How Caching Works:

- **Browser Caching**: Stores website data (like images, stylesheets, and scripts) in the user's browser for a set period, so returning visitors can load your site faster.
- **Server Caching**: Generates and stores static versions of dynamic content, reducing the processing load on your server.

Best Caching Plugins for WordPress:

1. **WP Rocket**:
   - User-friendly and powerful, WP Rocket is a premium caching plugin that offers robust performance optimization features.
   - Features include page caching, browser caching, lazy loading, and database optimization.
2. **W3 Total Cache**:
   - A free and comprehensive caching plugin that supports minification, database caching, and object caching.
3. **LiteSpeed Cache**:
   - Designed for websites hosted on LiteSpeed servers, it offers excellent caching and optimization features.

Setting Up Caching with WP Rocket:

1. Install and activate WP Rocket from your WordPress dashboard.

2. After activation, WP Rocket will automatically apply basic caching rules.

3. Navigate to **Settings > WP Rocket** to configure additional options:

   o **Cache Tab**: Enable mobile and logged-in user caching if necessary.

   o **File Optimization Tab**: Minify CSS, JavaScript, and HTML files to reduce file sizes.

   o **Media Tab**: Enable lazy loading for images and videos to improve load times.

Image Optimization: Reducing Image Sizes Without Losing Quality

Why Image Optimization Matters:

Images often make up the largest portion of a webpage's file size. Optimizing images can significantly improve load times without compromising visual quality.

Techniques for Image Optimization:

1. **Resize Images**:

   o Before uploading images, resize them to the exact dimensions required by your site. For example, a full-width hero image might need to be 1200px wide, while a thumbnail might only require 150px.

2. **Compress Images**:

   o Use tools or plugins to compress image file sizes without losing noticeable quality.

   o Popular tools include **TinyPNG**, **ImageOptim**, and **ShortPixel**.

3. **Use the Right Image Format**:

   o **JPEG**: Best for photographs.

   o **PNG**: Ideal for images that require transparency.

   o **WebP**: A modern format offering smaller file sizes without sacrificing quality.

Best Image Optimization Plugins for WordPress:

1. **Smush**:

   o Automatically compresses and optimizes images during upload.

   o Offers bulk optimization for existing images.

2. **ShortPixel**:

   o Compresses images and converts them to WebP format.

   o Includes a CDN option for even faster delivery.

3. **Imagify**:

   o Integrates seamlessly with WP Rocket, making it a great choice for combined optimization and caching.

Real-World Example: Speeding Up a WordPress Site Using WP Rocket and Optimizing Images

To demonstrate how to optimize a WordPress site for speed, let's walk through a real-world scenario for a blog with large image galleries and dynamic content.

Step 1: Install WP Rocket for Caching

1. Go to **Plugins > Add New** and install WP Rocket.
2. Activate WP Rocket, and it will immediately apply default caching rules.
3. Access **Settings > WP Rocket** to configure additional options:
   o Enable **Lazy Loading** for images and iframes to delay the loading of below-the-fold content.
   o Turn on **File Optimization** to minify CSS, JavaScript, and HTML files.

Step 2: Optimize Images

1. Install the **Smush** plugin to optimize and compress all existing images on the site.
   o Go to **Plugins > Add New** and search for "Smush."
   o Activate the plugin and navigate to **Smush > Bulk Smush** to compress existing images.

2. For future uploads, enable automatic compression in Smush's settings to ensure all new images are optimized before being displayed on the site.

Step 3: Test Site Performance

1. Use tools like **Google PageSpeed Insights** or **GTmetrix** to analyze your site's performance before and after implementing optimizations.
2. Compare load times, file sizes, and overall scores to verify the effectiveness of caching and image optimization.

Results:

- After applying WP Rocket and optimizing images, the site's load time is reduced by several seconds, providing a smoother user experience and improving SEO rankings.

In this chapter, we covered the essentials of optimizing your WordPress site for speed. Caching is a critical component that reduces server load and speeds up content delivery, and WP Rocket offers a user-friendly way to implement caching effectively. Image optimization further enhances performance by reducing file sizes without sacrificing quality.

By combining caching and image optimization, you can achieve a faster, more responsive WordPress site that improves user experience, engagement, and SEO rankings.

In the next chapter, we'll explore **WordPress SEO**, focusing on how to optimize your site for search engines to attract more organic traffic.

Chapter 13: SEO for WordPress Websites

Search Engine Optimization (SEO) is one of the most important aspects of running a successful WordPress website. Regardless of whether you're managing a blog, an online store, or a business website, SEO helps ensure your site ranks well on search engines like Google, Bing, and Yahoo. This chapter will cover the essential on-page SEO techniques, using SEO plugins like Yoast SEO, and provide a real-world example of optimizing a blog post for search engines.

On-Page SEO: Optimizing Content, Meta Tags, and URLs

On-page SEO refers to the practice of optimizing elements on your website to improve its rankings on search engines. It includes content, meta tags, image alt text, and URL structure. Here's how to get started:

1. Content Optimization

Content is the core of SEO. High-quality, relevant, and engaging content is key to attracting both search engines and users.

- **Keyword Research**: Before writing content, research keywords that your audience is searching for. Tools like

Google Keyword Planner, **Ubersuggest**, and **SEMrush** can help identify high-volume, low-competition keywords.

- **Keyword Placement**: Once you've selected your target keyword, place it strategically within your content. Here's where to include it:
  - **Title Tag**: The title of your page or post should contain your target keyword. Keep it under 60 characters for optimal display on search engines.
  - **Headings**: Use headings (H1, H2, H3, etc.) to organize your content. Include your keywords in these headings to improve SEO. Ensure the H1 tag is used for your main title and should include your focus keyword.
  - **Body Text**: Mention your focus keyword naturally throughout the body of the text. Don't overstuff it—use variations and related keywords to avoid keyword cannibalization.

2. Meta Tags Optimization

Meta tags are snippets of text that describe the content of a page. They appear in the HTML code and are used by search engines to understand the content.

- **Meta Title**: The meta title is what appears as the clickable headline in search engine results. Ensure that your meta title contains the main keyword and provides a compelling reason to click. Example: "10 Tips for Effective WordPress SEO in 2024."

- **Meta Description**: The meta description provides a brief of the page's content and appears below the title in search results. Keep it under 160 characters and include the main keyword. Example: "Learn 10 actionable tips to improve your WordPress SEO and boost traffic to your website."

3. URL Structure

URLs should be simple, clean, and descriptive. Search engines prefer URLs that contain keywords and are easy for users to read.

- **Keyword-Rich URL**: Ensure your URL includes your target keyword. For example: www.example.com/wordpress-seo-tips.

- **Avoid Unnecessary Characters**: WordPress can sometimes generate URLs with unnecessary characters (e.g., ?p=123). Customize the URL to be more user-friendly by navigating to **Settings > Permalinks** in your WordPress dashboard and selecting a "Post name" structure.

4. Image Optimization

Images can significantly impact your SEO. Ensure your images are optimized for fast loading and include descriptive alt text.

- **Image Alt Text**: Alt text describes what an image is about. Use relevant keywords in the alt text to improve SEO. For example: "WordPress SEO tips for beginners" instead of just "image1.jpg."

- **Compress Images**: Large image files slow down your website's loading time. Use tools like **Smush** or **TinyPNG** to compress and optimize images without losing quality.

5. Internal Linking

Internal links help connect pages and posts within your website. This improves the user experience and helps search engines crawl your site.

- **Anchor Text**: Use descriptive anchor text for internal links, so search engines understand the context of the linked page. For example, "For more WordPress SEO tips, check out our guide on optimizing WordPress plugins."

SEO Plugins: Using Tools Like Yoast SEO

Yoast SEO is one of the most popular and powerful SEO plugins for WordPress. It simplifies many SEO tasks and ensures that your content adheres to best SEO practices.

1. Installing Yoast SEO

- Navigate to **Plugins > Add New** from your WordPress dashboard.

- Search for **Yoast SEO** and click "Install Now" followed by "Activate."

2. Setting Up Yoast SEO

After installing Yoast, you'll need to configure it. The plugin provides a setup wizard that walks you through the basic configuration, including:

- **Site Type**: Choose whether your site is a blog, online store, or news site.
- **Title Settings**: Yoast lets you customize the title format for different content types (posts, pages, etc.).
- **Social Media Integration**: Connect Yoast to your social media profiles for better integration.

3. Using Yoast SEO to Optimize Posts and Pages

- **Focus Keyword**: For each post or page, you can set a focus keyword that Yoast will use to evaluate your content's optimization. The plugin provides feedback on how well your content is optimized for that keyword.
- **Readability Analysis**: Yoast also evaluates your content's readability, suggesting ways to improve sentence length, paragraph structure, and overall flow.
- **Snippet Preview**: Yoast generates a preview of how your post will look in search results. You can customize the meta title and description directly within the post editor.

4. Advanced Features of Yoast SEO

- **XML Sitemaps**: Yoast automatically generates an XML sitemap, helping search engines discover and index your content more efficiently.

- **Breadcrumbs**: Yoast makes it easy to add breadcrumbs to your site's navigation. Breadcrumbs help search engines understand the structure of your site and improve the user experience.

- **Schema Markup**: Yoast helps add structured data (Schema.org markup) to your pages, which can improve your visibility in search results.

Real-World Example: Optimizing a Blog Post for Search Engines

Let's walk through the process of optimizing a blog post titled **"10 Tips for Better WordPress SEO"** using the SEO techniques mentioned above.

1. Conduct Keyword Research

- **Keyword Tools**: Use tools like **Ubersuggest** to discover high-volume keywords. In this case, you might target the keyword "WordPress SEO tips" or "improve WordPress SEO."

- **Long-Tail Keywords**: Consider targeting long-tail keywords like "how to improve WordPress SEO in 2024" for less competition and higher conversion.

2. Optimize Content

- **Title Tag**: Make sure the title includes the focus keyword. Example: "10 Tips for Better WordPress SEO in 2024."
- **Headings**: Use relevant keywords in your H2 and H3 tags. For example:
  - o   H2: "Why WordPress SEO is Essential"
  - o   H3: "How to Optimize Your WordPress Site for Better Rankings"
- **Body Text**: Write high-quality, informative content around your focus keyword. For example, mention key tactics like using SEO plugins, optimizing meta tags, and improving site speed.

3. Meta Tags and URL

- **Meta Title**: "10 Tips for Better WordPress SEO | Improve Your Site's Rankings"
- **Meta Description**: "Discover 10 actionable tips to enhance your WordPress SEO, drive more traffic, and improve your site's search engine rankings in 2024."
- **URL**: Make sure the URL is short, clean, and contains the keyword: www.example.com/wordpress-seo-tips.

4. Internal Linking and External Links

- **Internal Linking**: Add links to other related blog posts, like "How to Choose the Best SEO Plugin for WordPress."
- **External Links**: Link to authoritative sources, such as Google's SEO guidelines, to improve your credibility.

5. Using Yoast SEO

- **Focus Keyword**: Set the focus keyword to "WordPress SEO tips."
- **Readability Check**: Use Yoast to ensure that your post is easy to read. Yoast might recommend breaking up long paragraphs or adding more transition words.
- **Snippet Preview**: Customize the snippet preview to make sure the title and description are optimized for clicks.

6. Image Optimization

- Add images related to WordPress SEO, and ensure they are optimized for fast loading. Use **alt text** like "WordPress SEO plugin settings" for SEO and accessibility.

In this chapter, we've covered the essential elements of SEO for WordPress websites, including content optimization, meta tag optimization, and URL structure. We've also explored how to use Yoast SEO to streamline the process of optimizing your WordPress site for search engines. The real-world example showed how to apply these SEO techniques to a blog post, helping you increase your chances of ranking higher on Google and other search engines.

In the next chapter, we'll explore how to enhance your WordPress site with e-commerce capabilities using **WooCommerce**, allowing you to sell products or services online.

Chapter 14: E-Commerce with WooCommerce

In the world of online business, WooCommerce is one of the most popular and flexible platforms for creating and managing e-commerce websites on WordPress. It allows you to transform your WordPress site into a fully functional online store, enabling you to sell physical and digital products, manage inventory, process payments, and more. In this chapter, we will guide you through the steps of setting up WooCommerce, managing products and orders, and provide a real-world example of building an online store for selling physical products.

Setting Up WooCommerce: Installing and Configuring an Online Store

WooCommerce is a plugin that integrates seamlessly with WordPress, making it easy to add e-commerce functionality to your website. Follow these steps to install and configure WooCommerce:

1. Installing WooCommerce

To get started, you need to install the WooCommerce plugin on your WordPress site. Here's how you can do it:

- **Log into your WordPress Dashboard**: Navigate to your WordPress admin area.
- **Go to Plugins > Add New**: In the plugin search bar, type **WooCommerce**.
- **Click Install Now**: Once the plugin appears, click **Install Now**, then click **Activate** to activate the plugin.

WooCommerce will guide you through a setup wizard after activation, helping you configure basic settings for your online store.

2. Basic WooCommerce Setup

The WooCommerce setup wizard will ask you for several details about your store. Here's what you need to configure during the initial setup:

- **Store Setup**: Set your country, currency, and preferred units (weight, dimensions, etc.).
- **Product Type**: Choose whether you want to sell physical products, digital products, or both.
- **Payment Methods**: Set up payment gateways such as **PayPal**, **Stripe**, or **bank transfer** to process transactions.
- **Shipping Options**: Configure shipping rates based on location, weight, or flat rate.
- **Tax Settings**: Choose whether you want to charge taxes and configure tax rules for your region.

WooCommerce also provides advanced options for handling product types, shipping methods, and payment systems. However, for now, let's focus on the essentials.

3. Selecting a WooCommerce-Compatible Theme

Although WooCommerce works with most WordPress themes, choosing a theme that is fully compatible with WooCommerce will make your life easier. Themes like **Storefront** (created by WooCommerce) or **Astra** are excellent choices for e-commerce websites, as they come with built-in compatibility for store features.

Managing Products and Orders

Once WooCommerce is set up, you can start adding products, managing inventory, and processing orders. Here's how you can manage each part of your e-commerce store:

1. Adding Products

WooCommerce makes it simple to add new products to your store. Follow these steps:

- **Go to Products > Add New**: From your WordPress Dashboard, navigate to **Products** and select **Add New**.
- **Product Title and Description**: Enter the product title (e.g., "Blue T-Shirt") and a detailed product description. You can use the block editor (Gutenberg) to format the description using text, images, and videos.

- **Product Data**: Below the description, you'll see the **Product Data** section. This is where you'll configure important details about the product:
  - **General**: Set the regular price, sale price, and tax status (whether the product is taxable or not).
  - **Inventory**: Enable stock management and enter the quantity available. You can also set low stock notifications here.
  - **Shipping**: Define the weight and dimensions of the product to calculate shipping costs.
  - **Attributes**: Add attributes such as size or color for variable products.
  - **Linked Products**: You can link related products, upsells, and cross-sells to encourage more purchases.
- **Product Image and Gallery**: Upload the main image for the product and additional images (if necessary) for a product gallery.
- **Publish**: Once all the information is entered, click **Publish** to make the product live on your store.

2. Managing Inventory

WooCommerce offers simple inventory management tools that help you track stock levels and manage product availability.

- **Inventory Settings**: In the **Product Data** section, you can enable **Stock Management**. WooCommerce will automatically reduce stock levels as customers make purchases.
- **Notifications**: You can set low stock notifications to alert you when inventory is running low. This can be configured under **WooCommerce > Settings > Products > Inventory**.

3. Processing Orders

WooCommerce simplifies the process of managing customer orders. Here's how you can handle incoming orders:

- **Go to WooCommerce > Orders**: This section displays all the orders placed on your store.
- **View Order Details**: Clicking on an order number opens the order details, including customer information, products purchased, order status, and payment details.
- **Order Statuses**: WooCommerce allows you to manage orders with different statuses:
  - **Pending Payment**: When an order is awaiting payment.
  - **Processing**: When the payment is received, and the product is being prepared for shipment.
  - **Completed**: When the product has been shipped and delivered.

- o **Cancelled**: When the customer or store owner cancels the order.
- o **Refunded**: When a refund has been issued.
- **Shipping**: If you offer physical products, you can generate shipping labels and track shipments directly from the order screen.

Real-World Example: Building an Online Store for Selling Physical Products

Let's walk through the creation of a simple online store for selling **T-shirts** on WordPress using WooCommerce.

1. Installing and Configuring WooCommerce

We'll start by installing WooCommerce on your WordPress site, following the steps above to complete the basic configuration (store location, currency, and payment methods).

2. Adding Products

You're selling T-shirts in different colors and sizes. Here's how you can add these products:

- **Product 1: Blue T-Shirt**:
  - o Title: "Blue T-Shirt"
  - o Description: "A stylish and comfortable blue T-shirt made from 100% cotton."

- Price: $19.99
- SKU: BLUE-001
- Inventory: 50 available.
- Images: Add images of the T-shirt from different angles.

- **Product 2: Red T-Shirt**:
  - Title: "Red T-Shirt"
  - Description: "A vibrant red T-shirt perfect for casual wear."
  - Price: $19.99
  - SKU: RED-001
  - Inventory: 40 available.
  - Images: Add images of the T-shirt from different angles.

You can add more products similarly and customize their details such as size, color, and material.

3. Configuring Shipping and Taxes

- Set up **flat-rate shipping** for domestic orders ($5 per order) and international shipping based on zones.
- Define **tax rules**: Set up tax rates for different regions (e.g., 10% sales tax for U.S. customers).

4. Setting up Payments

- Enable **PayPal** as a payment gateway for international customers.
- Enable **Stripe** for credit card payments.

5. Promoting Your Store

To help your store gain traction, consider using **SEO** best practices for product descriptions, images, and meta tags (as covered in the previous chapter on SEO). Additionally, integrate social media buttons to share products directly from the store.

In this chapter, we've walked through the essential steps of setting up and managing an online store using WooCommerce. From installation to configuring payment methods, adding products, managing inventory, and processing orders, WooCommerce makes it easy to run a full-fledged e-commerce site. The real-world example of building an online store for selling T-shirts highlights how to apply these features in practice.

In the next chapter, we will explore **WordPress Analytics and Tracking**, where we'll cover how to monitor site performance, track customer behavior, and measure e-commerce success with tools like Google Analytics.

Chapter 15: Building Custom WordPress Themes

Creating a custom WordPress theme allows you to have full control over your site's design and functionality. Whether you want a completely unique look or you need to tweak an existing theme to meet your needs, understanding the fundamental structure of WordPress themes and how to customize them is a vital skill for any WordPress developer.

In this chapter, we will dive into the key components that make up a WordPress theme, how to customize them, and provide a hands-on real-world example of building a simple blog theme from scratch.

Theme Structure: Understanding Template Files, Functions, and Styles

A WordPress theme is made up of several essential files that work together to control the look and functionality of your website. Let's explore the most important elements that make up a theme's structure.

1. Template Files

A WordPress theme contains various template files that determine how different parts of the website are displayed. These files include:

- **index.php**: The main template file. If no other file is specified for a page, WordPress will use index.php to display it.

- **header.php**: Contains the opening HTML and the code for the header section, typically including the site's title, navigation menu, and other elements common to every page.

- **footer.php**: Contains the closing HTML and the footer section, typically including copyright information, footer menus, and contact details.

- **single.php**: Used to display individual blog posts or pages.

- **page.php**: Used to display static pages.

- **archive.php**: Used to display archive pages, such as category, tag, and date-based archives.

- **functions.php**: A crucial file used to define theme-specific functionality, such as adding custom features or integrating third-party plugins.

- **style.css**: The main stylesheet of the theme, which dictates the visual design of the site. This file contains CSS rules for layout, typography, colors, etc.

The layout of a theme is determined by how these files work together. For example, header.php will include the site's navigation, while footer.php will include the footer links. These template files call each other through functions in functions.php.

2. Functions File (functions.php)

The functions.php file is where you add custom functions to extend the theme's functionality. For example, you can register new widget areas, enable support for post thumbnails, and enqueue stylesheets and scripts.

Some common functions added to functions.php include:

- **Adding Theme Support**: This is used to enable WordPress features like post thumbnails, custom logos, or menus.

  php

  ```php
  function my_theme_setup() {
      add_theme_support('post-thumbnails');
      add_theme_support('custom-logo');
      add_theme_support('menus');
  }
  add_action('after_setup_theme', 'my_theme_setup');
  ```

- **Enqueuing Scripts and Styles**: This allows you to properly add JavaScript and CSS files to your theme.

  php

```
function my_theme_scripts() {
  wp_enqueue_style('style', get_stylesheet_uri());
  wp_enqueue_script('jquery');
}
add_action('wp_enqueue_scripts', 'my_theme_scripts');
```

3. Stylesheet (style.css)

The style.css file contains the visual styles for the entire theme. It's where you define how elements like headers, paragraphs, and images will look on the front-end of your site.

You must also include a special comment at the top of the style.css file to define the theme's metadata:

css

```
/*
Theme Name: My Custom Theme
Theme URI: http://example.com/my-theme
Author: Your Name
Author URI: http://example.com
Description: A custom WordPress theme for my blog
Version: 1.0
License: GNU General Public License v2 or later
*/
```

Customizing Themes: Creating a Child Theme and Adding Custom Styles

While you can modify an existing theme directly, it's recommended to create a **child theme** instead. A child theme inherits the functionality of the parent theme but allows you to make customizations without affecting the original theme. If you update the parent theme, your changes won't be overwritten.

1. Creating a Child Theme

A child theme consists of two main files:

- **style.css**: A new style.css file, which imports styles from the parent theme.
- **functions.php**: An optional functions.php file to add additional functionality or override functions from the parent theme.

Here's how you can create a child theme:

1. **Create a new folder** for the child theme. Name it something like my-custom-theme-child.
2. Inside the folder, create a new style.css file. At the top of this file, add the following:

css

```
/*
Theme Name: My Custom Theme Child
Theme URI: http://example.com/my-custom-theme-child
Description: A child theme for My Custom Theme
Author: Your Name
```

Template: my-custom-theme

Version: 1.0

*/

The **Template** value must match the folder name of the parent theme.

3. Create a functions.php file to enqueue the parent theme's stylesheet:

php

```php
<?php
function my_custom_theme_child_enqueue_styles() {
    wp_enqueue_style('parent-style',    get_template_directory_uri()    .
'/style.css');
    wp_enqueue_style('child-style', get_stylesheet_uri(), array('parent-
style'));
}
add_action('wp_enqueue_scripts',
'my_custom_theme_child_enqueue_styles');
```

Once you've created these files, activate the child theme from the WordPress Dashboard under **Appearance > Themes**.

2. Adding Custom Styles

With the child theme in place, you can now add custom styles without modifying the parent theme. Open the style.css file in the child theme and add your custom CSS.

For example, if you want to change the background color of your blog:

css

```
body {
   background-color: #f0f0f0;
}
```

You can also override styles defined in the parent theme by writing more specific CSS rules.

3. Customizing Theme Templates

To customize template files (like header.php or footer.php), copy the file you want to modify from the parent theme to the child theme's folder. For example, if you want to modify the header.php file, copy it from the parent theme and paste it into the child theme's folder.

Now, you can edit the header.php file in the child theme without affecting the parent theme. WordPress will automatically use the child theme's file instead of the parent theme's file.

Real-World Example: Building a Simple Blog Theme from Scratch

Now that we understand the structure of WordPress themes and how to customize them, let's build a simple blog theme from scratch.

1. Setting Up the Theme Folder

First, create a new folder for your theme. Name it simple-blog-theme. Inside this folder, create the following files:

- **style.css** (with theme metadata)
- **index.php**
- **header.php**
- **footer.php**
- **functions.php**

2. Writing Basic Theme Files

- **style.css:**

css

```css
/*
Theme Name: Simple Blog Theme
Description: A simple blog theme for WordPress
Author: Your Name
Version: 1.0
*/
body {
    font-family: Arial, sans-serif;
    line-height: 1.6;
    background-color: #f4f4f4;
    margin: 0;
    padding: 0;
}
header {
```

```
    background-color: #333;
    color: #fff;
    padding: 20px;
    text-align: center;
}
```

- **header.php**:

php

```php
<!DOCTYPE html>
<html <?php language_attributes(); ?>>
<head>
    <meta charset="<?php bloginfo('charset'); ?>">
    <meta name="viewport" content="width=device-width, initial-scale=1.0">
    <title><?php bloginfo('name'); ?></title>
    <?php wp_head(); ?>
</head>
<body <?php body_class(); ?>>
<header>
    <h1><?php bloginfo('name'); ?></h1>
    <p><?php bloginfo('description'); ?></p>
</header>
```

- **footer.php**:

php

```php
<footer>
```

```
<p>&copy; <?php echo date("Y"); ?> My Simple Blog. All rights
reserved.</p>
</footer>
<?php wp_footer(); ?>
</body>
</html>
```

- **functions.php**:

php

```
function simple_blog_theme_enqueue_styles() {
    wp_enqueue_style('style', get_stylesheet_uri());
}
add_action('wp_enqueue_scripts',
'simple_blog_theme_enqueue_styles');
```

- **index.php**:

php

```
<?php get_header(); ?>

<div class="content">
    <h2>Latest Posts</h2>
    <?php
    if (have_posts()) :
        while (have_posts()) : the_post();
            ?>
            <h3><a href="<?php the_permalink(); ?>"><?php the_title();
?></a></h3>
```

```
    <p><?php the_excerpt(); ?></p>
    <?php
  endwhile;
 else :
   echo '<p>No posts found.</p>';
 endif;
 ?>
</div>

<?php get_footer(); ?>
```

3. Activate Your Theme

Once you've created these files, go to **Appearance > Themes** in your WordPress dashboard, and activate your new Simple Blog Theme. You should see a basic blog layout with the name and description of your site, as well as a list of recent posts.

Conclusion

In this chapter, we covered the essential structure of WordPress themes, how to create a child theme to customize a site safely, and how to build a simple blog theme from scratch. By understanding the basics of WordPress theme development, you can create custom designs that align with your vision, whether you're starting from a blank canvas or modifying an existing theme.

Chapter 16: Introduction to WordPress Custom Post Types (CPT)

WordPress started as a blogging platform, but over the years, it has evolved into a versatile content management system (CMS) capable of handling a wide variety of websites. One of the powerful features that contribute to this versatility is **Custom Post Types (CPTs)**. Custom Post Types allow you to extend the default content types (posts, pages, attachments) and create entirely new types of content that fit your site's unique needs.

In this chapter, we will explore what Custom Post Types are, why they are essential, how to create them using both code and plugins, and a real-world example to illustrate how you can use CPTs to build a portfolio section on your website.

What are Custom Post Types (CPT)?

By default, WordPress comes with several content types: posts, pages, attachments (media), revisions, and more. These are the content types WordPress uses to store and organize information. However, these built-in content types are not always enough for every project. For instance, a website for a restaurant might need a custom content type for "Menu Items," while a photographer's website might require a "Portfolio" content type.

A **Custom Post Type (CPT)** is a content type that you create to suit your website's needs. CPTs allow you to organize and display content in a way that is distinct from the default posts or pages.

Why Do You Need Custom Post Types?

Custom Post Types offer several benefits:

1. **Organizational Structure**: They help organize your content by separating it into distinct categories. For example, a real estate website might use CPTs for "Listings" and "Agents," while a news site might have "Articles," "Interviews," and "Press Releases."

2. **Custom Fields and Taxonomies**: Custom Post Types can be paired with **custom fields** (additional metadata) and **custom taxonomies** (custom categories or tags) to provide more granular control over how content is displayed and structured.

3. **Better Content Management**: Using CPTs makes it easier for site administrators to manage content because it's grouped into logical, meaningful sections.

4. **Improved SEO and User Experience**: With properly organized content, you can create more SEO-friendly URLs and provide users with an enhanced browsing experience, as your content is structured and categorized intuitively.

Creating Custom Post Types

There are two main ways to create Custom Post Types: by writing code or using a plugin. Let's go through both approaches.

1. Creating Custom Post Types with Code

You can register Custom Post Types in WordPress by using the register_post_type() function. This function is usually added to the functions.php file of your theme (or in a custom plugin for better portability). Here's an example of how you might register a CPT called "Portfolio":

php

```
function create_portfolio_cpt() {
  $args = array(
    'labels' => array(
      'name' => 'Portfolios',
      'singular_name' => 'Portfolio',
      'add_new' => 'Add New',
      'add_new_item' => 'Add New Portfolio Item',
      'edit_item' => 'Edit Portfolio Item',
      'new_item' => 'New Portfolio Item',
      'view_item' => 'View Portfolio Item',
      'search_items' => 'Search Portfolios',
      'not_found' => 'No portfolios found',
      'not_found_in_trash' => 'No portfolios found in Trash',
      'all_items' => 'All Portfolios',
      'archives' => 'Portfolio Archives',
    ),
```

```
    'public' => true,
    'show_in_menu' => true,
    'has_archive' => true,
    'rewrite' => array('slug' => 'portfolio'),
    'supports' => array('title', 'editor', 'thumbnail', 'excerpt'),
    'show_in_rest' => true, // Enable for Gutenberg editor
  );
  register_post_type('portfolio', $args);
}
add_action('init', 'create_portfolio_cpt');
```

In this code:

- We define the **labels** that will appear in the WordPress admin panel.
- We set 'public' => true, meaning this CPT will be publicly available and visible on the front-end of the website.
- The 'supports' array specifies what features the CPT should support, such as the title, editor (content), thumbnail, and excerpt.
- The 'rewrite' argument defines the custom slug for the CPT, so the URL for portfolio items will look like www.example.com/portfolio/item-name.

Once you've added this code to your theme's functions.php file, you'll be able to create and manage portfolio items directly from the WordPress admin panel.

2. Creating Custom Post Types with a Plugin

If you're not comfortable writing code or want a faster solution, there are several plugins available that simplify the process of creating CPTs. One popular plugin is **Custom Post Type UI (CPT UI)**. Here's how you can use it to create a Custom Post Type:

1. **Install the Plugin**: From your WordPress dashboard, go to **Plugins > Add New**, search for **Custom Post Type UI**, and install it.
2. **Activate the Plugin**: After installation, activate the plugin.
3. **Create a CPT**:
   - Go to **CPT UI > Add/Edit Post Types**.
   - In the **Post Type Slug** field, enter a slug for your custom post type (e.g., portfolio).
   - Fill in the labels and settings for your CPT, similar to how you'd do it with code.
   - Once done, click **Add Post Type**.

Now, your custom post type will be available, and you can begin adding portfolio items through the WordPress dashboard.

3. Customizing the Display of Custom Post Types

Once your Custom Post Type is created, you'll want to customize how it appears on the front-end of your website. By default, WordPress will display your CPT content using the same templates as posts or pages, but you can create custom templates specifically for your CPT.

For example, if you want to customize the display of your portfolio items, you can create a single-portfolio.php template file in your theme folder. WordPress will use this file to display individual portfolio items.

You can also create an archive template, such as archive-portfolio.php, to control how the portfolio listings appear when someone views all portfolio items.

Real-world Example: Building a Portfolio Section Using a Custom Post Type

Let's walk through a real-world example of creating a **Portfolio** section using a Custom Post Type for a photography website. Here's how you would go about doing it:

1. **Create the Portfolio Custom Post Type**: Follow the steps outlined earlier (either through code or the CPT UI plugin) to create a new Custom Post Type called **Portfolio**.

2. **Add Custom Fields (Optional)**: To make the portfolio items more informative, you might want to add custom fields. For example, you might add fields for "Client Name," "Project Date," and "Project Type." You can do this with a plugin like **Advanced Custom Fields (ACF)**.

3. **Customize the Templates**:

- o **single-portfolio.php**: This template will display each portfolio item. You might include the project's name, images, and custom fields such as the client's name and project description.

Example of single-portfolio.php:

php

```php
<?php get_header(); ?>
<div class="portfolio-item">
    <h1><?php the_title(); ?></h1>
    <div class="portfolio-description"><?php the_content(); ?></div>
    <div class="portfolio-meta">
        <strong>Client:</strong> <?php the_field('client_name'); ?><br>
        <strong>Project Date:</strong> <?php the_field('project_date'); ?>
    </div>
    <div class="portfolio-gallery">
        <?php the_post_thumbnail(); ?>
        <!-- Add gallery or images here -->
    </div>
</div>
<?php get_footer(); ?>
```

- o **archive-portfolio.php**: This template will display all portfolio items in a grid or list format. You can use get_posts() or WP_Query to fetch and display the portfolio items.

Example of archive-portfolio.php:

php

```php
<?php get_header(); ?>
<div class="portfolio-archive">
  <h1>Portfolio</h1>
  <?php
  $args = array(
    'post_type' => 'portfolio',
    'posts_per_page' => 10,
  );
  $query = new WP_Query($args);
  if ($query->have_posts()) :
    while ($query->have_posts()) : $query->the_post();
      ?>
      <div class="portfolio-item">
        <a href="<?php the_permalink(); ?>">
          <h2><?php the_title(); ?></h2>
          <?php the_post_thumbnail(); ?>
        </a>
      </div>
      <?php
    endwhile;
  else :
    echo '<p>No portfolio items found.</p>';
  endif;
  wp_reset_postdata();
  ?>
</div>
<?php get_footer(); ?>
```

4. **Display Portfolio Items on the Front-End**: Once the templates are in place, your portfolio section will be ready to showcase all your work. Simply add portfolio items via the WordPress admin panel, and they will appear according to the custom templates you've defined.

Conclusion

Custom Post Types (CPTs) are a powerful feature in WordPress that allow you to create and manage different types of content tailored to your site's needs. By creating CPTs, you can build organized, structured content that makes it easier for visitors to navigate and engage with your website.

In this chapter, we've covered the basics of creating and using Custom Post Types, both through code and plugins. We've also looked at a real-world example of how to build a **Portfolio** section on a website using a CPT. With this knowledge, you can now expand your WordPress site beyond simple posts and pages, giving it the flexibility to handle more complex content structures.

Chapter 17: Working with WordPress Custom Fields

Custom Fields are one of WordPress's most powerful features. They allow you to add extra metadata or content to posts, pages, and custom post types, giving you complete control over the structure and display of your content. These fields are often used to store additional information that doesn't fit into the default fields such as titles, content, or categories.

In this chapter, we will explore how to use **Custom Fields** and **Meta Boxes** to enhance your posts and pages. You will learn how to create, manage, and display custom fields, and we'll go through a real-world example of adding and displaying a custom field for a **product review**.

What are Custom Fields?

Custom Fields, also known as **post metadata**, allow you to attach additional information to a WordPress post, page, or custom post type. These fields can be used to store any kind of content, such as product prices, event dates, or even custom data like product reviews, client names, etc.

In simple terms, Custom Fields are key-value pairs that add more details to a post. The **key** is the name of the field (e.g., "Price,"

"Rating," "Location"), and the **value** is the content associated with that field (e.g., "$19.99," "5 stars," "New York").

Why Use Custom Fields?

1. **Customization**: You can add fields that are unique to your site or project. For instance, if you're building a product catalog, you might want to add custom fields for "Price," "Product Dimensions," or "Availability."

2. **Flexible Content Management**: Custom Fields allow for storing data that's not part of the default post content. This helps in creating more organized and structured content.

3. **SEO and User Experience**: By adding custom metadata, you can structure your content in a way that is more SEO-friendly and provides more useful information to your users.

Working with Custom Fields

1. Adding Custom Fields to Posts or Pages

Custom Fields are typically added through the WordPress **post editor**, where you can enter them manually for each post or page. Here's how you can add Custom Fields:

1. **Navigate to the Post or Page Editor**: In your WordPress dashboard, go to **Posts** or **Pages** and click on the post/page you want to edit.

2. **Enable Custom Fields (If Not Visible)**: If the Custom Fields section is not visible, scroll to the top of the editor and click the **Screen Options** tab. Check the box next to **Custom Fields** to make it visible.

3. **Add a Custom Field**: Once the Custom Fields box is visible, click on **Enter New**. You will need to specify the **Name** (key) and the **Value** for your custom field.
   - **Example**: If you're adding a product price, you might use:
     - **Name**: Price
     - **Value**: $19.99

4. **Save the Post/Page**: After adding the custom fields, save or update your post.

2. Using Meta Boxes for Custom Fields

Meta boxes are a more user-friendly way to manage Custom Fields. Instead of using the built-in Custom Fields panel, meta boxes allow developers to create custom content fields with different types of input fields like text boxes, dropdowns, checkboxes, and more.

Here's how to add a custom meta box for a post:

php

```
function add_custom_meta_box() {
  add_meta_box(
```

```php
        'product_review',        // Meta box ID
        'Product Review',        // Title
        'display_product_review',  // Callback function
        'post',                  // Post type where the meta box will appear
        'normal',                // Context (location)
        'high'                   // Priority
    );
}
add_action('add_meta_boxes', 'add_custom_meta_box');


function display_product_review($post) {
    // Nonce field for security
    wp_nonce_field('save_product_review', 'product_review_nonce');

    // Retrieve the current review data if it exists
    $rating = get_post_meta($post->ID, '_product_rating', true);
    ?>
    <label for="product_rating">Product Rating:</label>
    <input    type="number"    id="product_rating"    name="product_rating"
value="<?php echo esc_attr($rating); ?>" min="1" max="5" step="1">
    <?php
}


// Save custom field data
function save_product_review($post_id) {
    // Verify nonce
    if                 (!isset($_POST['product_review_nonce'])                 ||
!wp_verify_nonce($_POST['product_review_nonce'], 'save_product_review')) {
        return;
    }
```

```
// Save the product rating
if (isset($_POST['product_rating'])) {
    update_post_meta($post_id,                         '_product_rating',
sanitize_text_field($_POST['product_rating']));
  }
}
add_action('save_post', 'save_product_review');
```

In this example:

- A meta box titled **Product Review** is created and displayed on the post editor.
- A custom field (Product Rating) allows the user to enter a rating between 1 and 5.
- When the post is saved, the value is stored in the post's metadata using update_post_meta().

3. Displaying Custom Fields on the Frontend

Once you've added custom fields or meta boxes, you'll likely want to display that data on the front-end of your site. To do this, you'll use WordPress template tags like get_post_meta() to retrieve the data and display it within your theme files.

Let's take the **product review** example from earlier. To display the custom field data (e.g., the product rating) on a product page or blog post, you would add the following code to the appropriate template file:

php

```php
<?php
// Get the product rating for the current post
$product_rating = get_post_meta(get_the_ID(), '_product_rating', true);

// Check if a rating exists
if ($product_rating) {
    echo '<p>Product Rating: ' . esc_html($product_rating) . ' out of 5 stars</p>';
}
?>
```

In this code:

- get_post_meta() retrieves the value of the custom field based on the current post ID.
- We use esc_html() to safely display the rating and prevent XSS (Cross-site Scripting) vulnerabilities.

Real-world Example: Adding and Displaying a Custom Field for a Product Review

Let's walk through a complete example where we add and display a **product review** on a WordPress product page.

1. **Create a Custom Meta Box for Product Reviews**: Using the code provided earlier, we'll add a meta box where users can enter a **rating** for a product (e.g., a rating from 1 to 5 stars).

2. **Save the Review Data**: When a user submits the post with the rating, we save the data using update_post_meta(), so it is stored in the post's metadata.

3. **Display the Review on the Front-End**: We modify the single product page template to retrieve the rating and display it where it's relevant (e.g., under the product description).

The result is a product page that not only showcases the product but also displays a rating provided by the author. This is extremely useful for e-commerce sites or review-based blogs.

Conclusion

Custom Fields and Meta Boxes are powerful tools that allow you to store and display custom data associated with your posts, pages, and custom post types. Whether you're creating an online store, a portfolio, or a product review site, Custom Fields can be used to manage a wide range of content.

In this chapter, we've covered:

- What Custom Fields are and how they help in storing additional data.
- How to add Custom Fields manually through the editor or by using Meta Boxes.

- How to display this custom data on the front-end of your site.

- A real-world example of adding a product review and displaying it on a product page.

With Custom Fields, you can add virtually any type of custom content to your site, making it more versatile and personalized for your audience. This opens up new possibilities for your WordPress development projects.

Chapter 18: Introduction to WordPress REST API

The **REST API** (Representational State Transfer Application Programming Interface) is a powerful tool that allows WordPress to communicate and interact with other applications, services, and platforms. It extends WordPress beyond just a content management system by enabling external apps to retrieve, create, update, and delete content on a WordPress site. Whether you're building a mobile app, an external service integration, or a custom frontend, the WordPress REST API makes it easier to connect with WordPress data programmatically.

In this chapter, we'll dive into the basics of the WordPress REST API, how it works, and explore some real-world examples of how to interact with your WordPress data. By the end of this chapter, you'll have a solid understanding of how to retrieve data from your WordPress site and even build a simple frontend app that fetches content using the API.

What is the REST API?
The WordPress REST API is a set of HTTP endpoints that allow external applications to interact with your WordPress site. It enables you to send and receive data in formats like JSON

(JavaScript Object Notation), which is easy for both machines and humans to process.

The REST API allows WordPress to:

- Retrieve site content, including posts, pages, custom post types, and media files.
- Add new content (e.g., creating new posts, pages, or comments).
- Update existing content.
- Delete content from the site.
- Perform various other actions such as user management, taxonomy handling, and more.

The REST API is built into WordPress by default (since version 4.7), and it uses the same HTTP request methods that are common in web development: GET, POST, PUT, DELETE.

- **GET**: Retrieve data (e.g., fetching a post or list of posts).
- **POST**: Send data (e.g., creating a new post).
- **PUT**: Update existing data (e.g., updating a post).
- **DELETE**: Remove data (e.g., deleting a post).

How the REST API Works

The REST API works through **routes** and **endpoints**. A **route** is a URL that points to a specific function or resource in WordPress, while an **endpoint** is the actual request that corresponds to a particular operation (like retrieving posts, creating a post, etc.).

For example:

- **GET /wp-json/wp/v2/posts**: This retrieves a list of posts from the WordPress site.
- **GET /wp-json/wp/v2/posts/{id}**: This retrieves a specific post by its ID.
- **POST /wp-json/wp/v2/posts**: This creates a new post.

These routes provide a structured way to interact with WordPress data via HTTP requests.

Making API Requests

To make API requests, you typically use an HTTP client. This can be done from your web browser, from JavaScript (using fetch or libraries like Axios), or from any other external application that can make HTTP requests.

Here's a basic breakdown of how you can make a request to the WordPress REST API:

1. Retrieving Data (GET Request)

Let's say you want to retrieve all the posts from your WordPress site. You can make a simple GET request to the following endpoint:

bash

GET /wp-json/wp/v2/posts

This will return a JSON object with the data of the posts.

Example using **JavaScript** and fetch:

javascript

```
fetch('https://yourwebsite.com/wp-json/wp/v2/posts')
  .then(response => response.json())
  .then(data => {
    console.log(data); // The data from the WordPress site
  })
  .catch(error => console.log('Error fetching data:', error));
```

2. Creating Data (POST Request)

To create a new post via the API, you would use a POST request. For example, to create a new post, you would send a request like this:

bash

POST /wp-json/wp/v2/posts

The request body would contain the data you want to send, like the post's title and content:

javascript

```
const postData = {
  title: 'New Post',
```

```
content: 'This is the content of the new post.',
status: 'publish'  // 'draft' for drafts, 'publish' to make it live
};


fetch('https://yourwebsite.com/wp-json/wp/v2/posts', {
  method: 'POST',
  headers: {
   'Content-Type': 'application/json',
   'Authorization': 'Bearer YOUR_ACCESS_TOKEN'
  },
  body: JSON.stringify(postData)
})
  .then(response => response.json())
  .then(data => {
   console.log('New Post Created:', data);  // New post details
  })
  .catch(error => console.log('Error creating post:', error));
```

In this example, YOUR_ACCESS_TOKEN is a token that authenticates your request, ensuring that only authorized users can create or modify content.

3. Updating Data (PUT Request)

You can also update existing content using a PUT request. For example, if you want to update the title of a specific post, you would use:

bash

```
PUT /wp-json/wp/v2/posts/{id}
javascript
```

```
const updatedPostData = {
  title: 'Updated Title'
};


fetch('https://yourwebsite.com/wp-json/wp/v2/posts/123', { // 123 is the post ID
  method: 'PUT',
  headers: {
    'Content-Type': 'application/json',
    'Authorization': 'Bearer YOUR_ACCESS_TOKEN'
  },
  body: JSON.stringify(updatedPostData)
})
  .then(response => response.json())
  .then(data => {
    console.log('Post Updated:', data);
  })
  .catch(error => console.log('Error updating post:', error));
```

Real-world Example: Building a Simple Frontend App that Fetches Data from WordPress Using REST API

In this example, let's build a simple **frontend application** that fetches and displays the latest posts from a WordPress site using the REST API. We'll use **HTML**, **CSS**, and **JavaScript** to make the request and display the posts.

Step 1: Set Up Your HTML

html

```html
<!DOCTYPE html>
<html lang="en">
<head>
  <meta charset="UTF-8">
  <meta name="viewport" content="width=device-width, initial-scale=1.0">
  <title>WordPress Blog Posts</title>
  <style>
    body { font-family: Arial, sans-serif; }
    .post { margin-bottom: 20px; }
    .title { font-size: 24px; color: #333; }
    .content { font-size: 16px; color: #555; }
  </style>
</head>
<body>
  <h1>Latest Blog Posts</h1>
  <div id="posts-container"></div>

  <script src="app.js"></script>
</body>
</html>
```

Step 2: Fetch Data Using JavaScript (app.js)

javascript

```javascript
const postsContainer = document.getElementById('posts-container');

// Fetch data from WordPress REST API
fetch('https://yourwebsite.com/wp-json/wp/v2/posts')
  .then(response => response.json())
  .then(posts => {
    // Loop through the posts and display them
```

```
posts.forEach(post => {
  const postElement = document.createElement('div');
  postElement.classList.add('post');
  postElement.innerHTML = `
    <h2 class="title">${post.title.rendered}</h2>
    <div class="content">${post.excerpt.rendered}</div>
  `;
  postsContainer.appendChild(postElement);
});
})
.catch(error => console.error('Error fetching posts:', error));
```

Explanation:

- **HTML**: Creates the structure of the page with a container to display posts.
- **JavaScript**: Fetches the posts from the WordPress site using the REST API. It loops through the posts and displays their title and excerpt on the page.

Conclusion

The WordPress REST API opens up a whole new world of possibilities for interacting with your WordPress data programmatically. It allows you to build custom applications that can fetch, create, and update content without requiring direct interaction with the WordPress admin panel. Whether you're building a mobile app, an external service integration, or a custom frontend app, the REST API is an essential tool for WordPress developers.

In this chapter, we've covered:

- What the WordPress REST API is and how it works.
- How to make API requests to retrieve, create, update, and delete data.
- A real-world example of building a frontend app that fetches and displays WordPress posts using the REST API.

The REST API is an indispensable tool for modern WordPress development, allowing you to extend the functionality of your site and integrate it with external applications.

Chapter 19: Troubleshooting WordPress

When working with WordPress, it's inevitable that you'll run into problems or errors from time to time. Whether it's a plugin causing issues, themes not working as expected, or even a site that's completely down, being able to identify and troubleshoot common WordPress issues is an essential skill for any developer or website owner. In this chapter, we'll cover the most common WordPress errors, how to debug your site, and real-world examples of troubleshooting methods.

Common WordPress Errors: How to Identify and Resolve Common Issues

Here are some of the most common WordPress issues you might encounter:

1. **White Screen of Death (WSOD)**
   - **What it is**: The "White Screen of Death" happens when a WordPress site appears blank with no error messages. This can be caused by plugin conflicts, theme issues, or PHP errors.
   - **How to fix it**:
     - **Disable plugins**: Deactivate all plugins by renaming the plugins folder via FTP (wp-content/plugins) and check if the site loads. If

it does, reactivate each plugin one by one to identify the culprit.

- **Switch to default theme**: If deactivating plugins doesn't help, switch to a default WordPress theme (like Twenty Twenty-Three) to rule out theme-related issues.

- **Increase PHP memory limit**: Sometimes, a lack of memory can cause this issue. Add the following code to your wp-config.php file:

php

```
define('WP_MEMORY_LIMIT', '256M');
```

2. **Error Establishing a Database Connection**

   o **What it is**: This error usually appears when WordPress cannot connect to the database, typically due to incorrect database credentials or database server issues.

   o **How to fix it**:

     - Check the wp-config.php file for correct database credentials (DB_NAME, DB_USER, DB_PASSWORD, DB_HOST).

     - Ensure your database server is running and accessible. If your hosting provider is experiencing issues, contact them for assistance.

- You can also try repairing the database by adding the following line to wp-config.php:

php

define('WP_ALLOW_REPAIR', true);

Then visit http://yoursite.com/wp-admin/maint/repair.php to repair and optimize the database.

3. **404 Errors on Pages or Posts**
   - **What it is**: A 404 error occurs when a page or post cannot be found, even though it exists.
   - **How to fix it**:
     - Go to **Settings > Permalinks** and click **Save Changes** to flush the rewrite rules.
     - If you've recently changed permalinks or moved content, try resetting your permalinks to the default structure (/?p=123), then switch back to your preferred structure.

4. **Internal Server Error (500)**
   - **What it is**: A 500 Internal Server Error can be caused by a variety of issues such as a corrupt

.htaccess file, incompatible plugins, or exhausted PHP limits.

- o **How to fix it**:
  - **Deactivate all plugins**: Deactivate plugins one by one to identify the one causing the issue.
  - **Check the .htaccess file**: If the .htaccess file is corrupt, you can rename it (e.g., .htaccess_old) and WordPress will generate a new one. Alternatively, regenerate it by going to **Settings > Permalinks** and clicking **Save Changes**.
  - **Increase PHP limits**: Add the following to your wp-config.php to increase the PHP limit:

    php

    ```
    @ini_set( 'upload_max_size' , '64M' );
    @ini_set( 'max_execution_time' , '300' );
    @ini_set( 'max_input_time' , '300' );
    ```

5. **Plugin or Theme Compatibility Issues**
   - o **What it is**: Sometimes plugins and themes conflict with each other, causing errors or breaking your site.
   - o **How to fix it**:
     - **Deactivate all plugins** and switch to the default WordPress theme. If the issue

resolves, reactivate each plugin and theme one by one to identify the conflict.

- **Update plugins and themes**: Ensure all plugins and themes are updated to their latest versions.
- **Check plugin and theme documentation**: Some plugins or themes may require specific versions of WordPress or other plugins to function properly.

Debugging Tools: Using WP Debugging and Error Logs

When something goes wrong on your WordPress site, debugging is key. WordPress comes with several built-in debugging tools that can help identify the root cause of errors.

1. **WP_DEBUG**: Enabling WP_DEBUG in WordPress will display PHP errors, warnings, and notices directly on your site. This is useful for identifying issues in the code.
   - **How to enable WP_DEBUG**:
     1. Open your wp-config.php file.
     2. Add the following lines of code just above the line that says "That's all, stop editing! Happy blogging":

        php

```
define( 'WP_DEBUG', true );
define( 'WP_DEBUG_LOG', true );
define( 'WP_DEBUG_DISPLAY', false );
```

- WP_DEBUG: Enables WordPress debugging.
- WP_DEBUG_LOG: Logs errors to a file named debug.log located in the /wp-content/ directory.
- WP_DEBUG_DISPLAY: Disables displaying errors on the front-end of the site (good for live sites). Errors are still logged in the debug.log file.

Note: Always turn off debugging on live sites (by setting WP_DEBUG to false) to prevent exposing sensitive information.

2. **Error Logs**: WordPress error logs provide a detailed record of what went wrong, including database errors, PHP errors, and more. If your site isn't loading properly, check the debug.log file in the /wp-content/ directory for error messages that can help pinpoint the issue.

3. **Browser Developer Tools**: In addition to WordPress-specific debugging tools, you can use your browser's developer tools to troubleshoot frontend issues like JavaScript errors, CSS problems, and network requests. In Chrome, you can access this by pressing Ctrl + Shift + I

(Windows) or Cmd + Option + I (Mac) to open the developer console.

Real-world Example: Troubleshooting a WordPress Site That's Down Due to a Plugin Conflict

Imagine you have a WordPress site where everything was working fine, but suddenly, the site goes down, and all you see is a white screen (White Screen of Death). You suspect a plugin conflict but aren't sure which one is causing the problem.

Here's how you can troubleshoot:

1. **Disable All Plugins**:
    - Access your site's files via FTP or file manager.
    - Navigate to the wp-content directory and rename the plugins folder to something like plugins_old.
    - This will deactivate all plugins. If the site comes back up, you know the issue is plugin-related.
2. **Reactivate Plugins One by One**:
    - Rename the plugins_old folder back to plugins.
    - Go to the WordPress admin dashboard, and reactivate each plugin one by one, checking your site after each activation to identify which plugin causes the issue.
3. **Check for Plugin Updates**:

- o Once you find the problematic plugin, check for updates. Often, plugin developers release bug fixes for compatibility issues.
- o If no update is available, try deactivating the plugin and looking for an alternative or contact the plugin's support team.

4. **Switch to a Default Theme**:
   - o If disabling plugins doesn't solve the issue, try switching to a default WordPress theme (like Twenty Twenty-Three) to rule out a theme conflict.

5. **Enable Debugging**:
   - o If the issue persists, enable WP_DEBUG as mentioned earlier to display or log errors. Check the debug.log file for clues on what's going wrong.

Conclusion

Troubleshooting WordPress issues can sometimes be a frustrating process, but with the right tools and strategies, it becomes manageable. By understanding common errors, using debugging tools like WP_DEBUG, and following a systematic approach to diagnosing problems, you can quickly resolve issues and get your site back on track.

In this chapter, we covered:

- Common WordPress errors, their causes, and how to fix them.
- Essential debugging tools like WP_DEBUG and error logs.
- A real-world example of troubleshooting a plugin conflict that caused a site to go down.

By mastering WordPress troubleshooting, you'll be able to efficiently identify and resolve issues, ensuring your WordPress site runs smoothly and reliably.

Chapter 20: WordPress Maintenance and Updates

Maintaining and updating your WordPress site is essential to ensuring it remains secure, functional, and performs well over time. In this final chapter, we'll explore the importance of regular updates, provide a comprehensive site maintenance checklist, and walk through a real-world example of setting up a site maintenance schedule for a client's website.

***

Keeping WordPress Up to Date: How to Handle Core, Theme, and Plugin Updates

WordPress regularly releases updates to the core software, themes, and plugins. These updates may include bug fixes, new features, security patches, and performance improvements. Keeping everything up to date is crucial for ensuring the security and smooth functioning of your site.

1. **Core Updates**:
   o **Automatic Updates**: By default, WordPress automatically updates to the latest minor version (e.g., from 6.1.1 to 6.1.2). However, major updates (e.g., from 6.0 to 6.1) may require manual intervention.

- o **How to Update**: To manually update WordPress, navigate to **Dashboard > Updates** and click the **Update Now** button. You can also enable automatic updates for major releases by adding the following code to your wp-config.php file:

php

define('WP_AUTO_UPDATE_CORE', true);

This will ensure your site is always running the latest version of WordPress, reducing the risk of security vulnerabilities.

2. **Theme Updates**:
   - o **How to Update**: Like plugins, themes can be updated directly from the WordPress dashboard. Go to **Appearance > Themes**, and if a theme has an update available, you'll see a notification with the option to update. Always make sure to back up your site before updating themes, especially if you have made customizations to the theme files.
   - o **Child Themes**: If you've made customizations to a theme, it's a good practice to use a **child theme**. This prevents your customizations from being overwritten when the parent theme is updated.

3. **Plugin Updates**:

o **How to Update**: Plugins are updated through the **Plugins > Installed Plugins** menu. Similar to themes, WordPress will notify you if any plugins need updates. Click the **Update Now** button next to the plugin you want to update.

o **Important Notes**:

- Always update plugins one at a time to avoid potential conflicts.

- If a plugin update causes issues, consider restoring a backup or deactivating the plugin until a fix is released.

4. **Updating PHP Version**:

o Ensure your WordPress site runs on the latest supported version of PHP. Newer PHP versions offer improved performance and security. Check your hosting provider's control panel to see which PHP version is currently running and consider upgrading if it's outdated.

Site Maintenance Checklist: Regular Tasks for a Healthy WordPress Site

Maintaining a WordPress site isn't just about updating software. There are a number of other tasks that should be done regularly to keep your site performing well and free from errors. Here's a site maintenance checklist to follow:

1. **Backup Your Site**:
   o **Frequency**: Backup your site at least once a week (more frequently for high-traffic sites).
   o **Tools**: Use plugins like UpdraftPlus or BackupBuddy for automated backups, or take manual backups via your hosting provider's control panel.

2. **Test Site Backups**:
   o **Ensure Backups Work**: Regularly test your backups by restoring them to a staging site to ensure they're complete and functional.

3. **Update WordPress, Themes, and Plugins**:
   o **Frequency**: Check for updates weekly or when notified of new versions.
   o **Security Patches**: Apply security updates as soon as they're available to protect your site from vulnerabilities.

4. **Clear Cache**:
   o **Why**: Cached files can slow down your site or cause it to display outdated content. Regularly clearing the cache ensures that visitors see the latest version of your site.

o **Tools**: Use caching plugins like W3 Total Cache or WP Rocket to manage and clear cache.

5. **Optimize Your Database**:

   o **Why**: Over time, your database may accumulate unnecessary data (like post revisions, spam comments, and transients), which can slow down your site.

   o **How to Optimize**: Use plugins like WP-Optimize or WP-Sweep to clean and optimize your database. Alternatively, you can optimize your database manually using phpMyAdmin.

6. **Check Site Speed**:

   o **Why**: Site speed is critical for user experience and SEO. Regularly check your site's loading time.

   o **Tools**: Use Google PageSpeed Insights, GTmetrix, or Pingdom to analyze and improve your site's performance.

7. **Test Forms and Contact Pages**:

   o **Why**: Ensure all forms (contact, registration, etc.) are working correctly, as broken forms can lead to lost leads and frustrated users.

   o **How**: Regularly submit test entries through all forms to ensure they function properly and that you're receiving submissions.

8. **Monitor Site Security**:

- o **Why**: Ensure your site is protected from hacking attempts, malware, and spam.
- o **Tools**: Use security plugins like Wordfence or Sucuri to monitor and safeguard your site. Regularly scan for vulnerabilities and remove any suspicious files.

9. **Check for Broken Links**:
   - o **Why**: Broken links can harm user experience and SEO.
   - o **Tools**: Use plugins like Broken Link Checker to identify and fix broken links on your site.

10. **Review Analytics**:
    - o **Why**: Regularly check your site's traffic and performance using tools like Google Analytics or Jetpack. This helps identify areas for improvement.
    - o **What to Look For**: Monitor traffic patterns, bounce rates, and user behavior to optimize your content and improve user engagement.

Real-world Example: Setting Up a Site Maintenance Schedule for a Client's Site

Let's walk through an example of how you might set up a site maintenance schedule for a client's WordPress website. Imagine your client has a small e-commerce store running on WordPress with WooCommerce.

1. **Initial Setup**:
   - o **Frequency**: You agree to perform monthly maintenance for the client, with weekly checks for security updates.
   - o **Tasks**: Every month, you'll update the WordPress core, themes, and plugins. You'll also back up the entire site, optimize the database, and test the site's speed.

2. **Backup Schedule**:
   - o **Automated Backups**: You set up automated backups with a plugin like UpdraftPlus to ensure daily backups.
   - o **Manual Backups**: On the first Monday of each month, you manually perform a full backup and store it on an off-site location (like Google Drive or Dropbox).

3. **Performance Checks**:
   - o **Tools**: On the first Wednesday of each month, you'll check the site's speed using GTmetrix and Google PageSpeed Insights. You'll fix any performance issues identified by the reports.

- o **Content Optimization**: You'll work with the client to optimize images and content every quarter to keep the site's loading time down.

4. **Plugin and Theme Updates**:

    - o **Frequency**: You'll check for updates every Monday and apply security updates immediately.

    - o **Manual Updates**: For major updates (like WooCommerce or WordPress core updates), you'll test on a staging site before applying them to the live site.

5. **Security Checks**:

    - o **Tools**: You use Wordfence for daily security scans, and you'll perform a manual check of the site's security every month. This includes checking for malware, ensuring SSL is active, and reviewing user roles and permissions.

6. **Reporting**:

    - o **Monthly Reports**: At the end of each month, you provide the client with a detailed report outlining all updates, backups, performance improvements, and security checks completed.

By setting up this regular maintenance schedule, you ensure that the site stays secure, fast, and functional, which builds trust with your client and helps them avoid potential issues down the line.

Conclusion

Regular WordPress maintenance is vital to the long-term success of a website. By staying on top of core, theme, and plugin updates, and performing essential tasks like backups, security checks, and performance optimizations, you can ensure that your WordPress site continues to perform at its best.

In this chapter, we covered:

- The importance of keeping WordPress, themes, and plugins up to date.
- A comprehensive maintenance checklist for ensuring a healthy WordPress site.
- A real-world example of setting up a site maintenance schedule for a client's site.

By implementing these best practices and staying consistent with maintenance, you'll keep your WordPress site secure, efficient, and ready for growth.

Chapter 21: WordPress and SEO: Optimizing Your Website for Search Engines

In today's digital landscape, search engine optimization (SEO) is a crucial element in ensuring the visibility and success of a WordPress website. SEO involves a range of techniques and strategies that aim to improve a website's ranking on search engines like Google, making it more discoverable by potential visitors. This chapter will guide you through understanding SEO for WordPress, implementing essential optimization techniques, and leveraging the right tools to enhance your website's performance in search engine results.

Introduction to WordPress SEO

Why SEO is Important for WordPress Websites

SEO is not just about adding keywords to your content; it's about creating a comprehensive strategy to improve your website's search engine rankings. For WordPress websites, SEO plays an even more significant role because WordPress is widely used for blogging, e-commerce, and other types of content-heavy websites. Without proper optimization, even the best-designed website might not reach its target audience.

Key reasons why SEO is essential for WordPress:

- **Increased Visibility**: A well-optimized website will rank higher in search results, making it more likely to be discovered by users searching for relevant topics.
- **Higher Organic Traffic**: Organic search traffic remains one of the most sustainable and cost-effective ways to attract visitors.
- **Better User Experience**: Good SEO practices lead to faster load times, improved mobile compatibility, and easier navigation, enhancing the overall user experience.
- **Competitive Advantage**: Effective SEO will help you outrank your competitors, gaining an edge in search engine visibility.

Overview of SEO Basics: Keywords, On-page SEO, and Technical SEO

1. **Keywords**: Keywords are the foundation of SEO. They are the terms or phrases users type into search engines to find content. For WordPress sites, keyword research helps determine which terms will bring the most relevant traffic.
   - **Real-world Example**: Using a tool like Google Keyword Planner or Ubersuggest, a food blog might target the keyword "easy vegan recipes" to attract readers interested in plant-based cooking.

2. **On-page SEO**: This refers to the optimization of individual pages of your website to improve their ranking. It includes elements like:

    o   **Meta Descriptions**: Short descriptions that appear under page titles in search results.

    o   **Title Tags**: The main title displayed in search results and browser tabs.

    o   **Header Tags**: These tags organize content and help search engines understand the structure of your page.

    o   **Image Alt Text**: Descriptions of images for accessibility and SEO.

    o   **URL Structure**: Clean, keyword-rich URLs are easier for search engines to index.

3. **Technical SEO**: This involves optimizing the technical aspects of your website, such as site speed, mobile-friendliness, secure HTTPS protocols, and the creation of XML sitemaps.

    o   **Real-world Example**: Improving a website's load time by optimizing images, using caching plugins, and minifying CSS/JavaScript files.

Using Plugins for SEO

WordPress offers numerous plugins to help optimize your website for search engines. The most popular plugins for SEO are **Yoast SEO** and **Rank Math**. These plugins make SEO tasks more manageable by providing easy-to-understand suggestions and automatically handling some of the more complex technical aspects.

Setting Up and Configuring Popular SEO Plugins like Yoast SEO or Rank Math

1. **Yoast SEO**:
   - **Installation and Setup**: After installing Yoast, you'll be guided through the initial setup process, including configuring your website's title, meta description, and social profiles.
   - **On-Page Optimization**: Yoast provides a simple interface where you can enter the focus keyword for each page and get feedback on how to optimize your content.
   - **XML Sitemaps**: Yoast automatically generates an XML sitemap for your site, making it easier for search engines to index your pages.
   - **Real-world Example**: For a blog post about "best travel destinations," Yoast will suggest improvements such as including internal links,

using the keyword in subheadings, and adding related images with alt text.

2. **Rank Math**:

   o **Installation and Setup**: Similar to Yoast, Rank Math offers a setup wizard that configures the basic SEO settings of your website.

   o **Advanced Features**: Rank Math also includes advanced features such as schema markup, redirection management, and integration with Google Search Console.

   o **Real-world Example**: For an e-commerce store, Rank Math can optimize product pages by suggesting how to use keywords in titles, descriptions, and images for better product visibility.

Advanced SEO Strategies

Optimizing for Speed and Mobile-Friendliness

Search engines prioritize websites that load quickly and are mobile-friendly. Google's Core Web Vitals have made site speed and mobile responsiveness important ranking factors.

- **Improving Website Speed**:

  o **Caching**: Install caching plugins like **W3 Total Cache** or **WP Super Cache** to serve cached

versions of your pages, which significantly reduce loading times.

- o **Image Optimization**: Use plugins like **Smush** or **ShortPixel** to compress images without sacrificing quality.
- o **Minify CSS and JavaScript**: Tools like **Autoptimize** can help reduce file sizes and improve load times.

- **Mobile-Friendliness**:
  - o Make sure your WordPress theme is mobile-responsive, meaning it adjusts properly to different screen sizes. Many modern themes are built with mobile-first design in mind.
  - o Test mobile performance using **Google's Mobile-Friendly Test** tool.

- **Real-world Example**: A local bakery's website uses image optimization plugins to compress their product photos and a caching plugin to serve faster content, resulting in a noticeable reduction in bounce rates.

Implementing Structured Data (Schema Markup) to Enhance Rich Snippets

Structured data helps search engines understand the content of your website and can lead to enhanced results like rich snippets, which display additional information in search results.

- **What is Schema Markup?**: Schema markup is a type of code you can add to your website's HTML that defines specific content types (e.g., articles, products, reviews) for search engines.

- **Real-world Example**: For a recipe website, adding schema markup for recipes allows search engines to display key information such as cook time, ratings, and ingredients directly in search results.

SEO Reporting and Analytics

How to Use Google Analytics and Search Console for SEO Tracking

1. **Google Analytics**:
   - **Setting Up Goals**: Track conversions like newsletter sign-ups or product purchases.
   - **Behavior Flow**: Understand how users navigate through your site to identify areas that need improvement.
   - **Real-world Example**: Using Google Analytics, a WordPress blogger tracks the source of their traffic, identifying that social media is a primary driver of visits.

2. **Google Search Console**:

- o **Submit Sitemaps**: Ensure Google is properly indexing your site by submitting XML sitemaps.
- o **Monitor Performance**: Track clicks, impressions, and average position for targeted keywords.
- o **Fix Errors**: Google Search Console helps identify and resolve issues like crawl errors and broken links.

Real-World Example: Setting Up SEO Dashboards and Reviewing Performance

- **Creating SEO Dashboards**: Use Google Data Studio to create custom SEO dashboards that pull data from Google Analytics and Google Search Console. This gives you an at-a-glance view of your site's performance.
- **Tracking SEO Performance**: Regularly check keyword rankings, organic traffic growth, and user engagement metrics to identify what's working and what needs adjustment.

---

s:

- SEO is a multi-faceted approach that includes on-page, technical, and off-page strategies.
- WordPress offers several plugins, such as Yoast SEO and Rank Math, that simplify the process of optimization.

- Advanced SEO techniques, such as optimizing for speed, mobile-friendliness, and implementing structured data, can significantly enhance your site's visibility and user experience.
- Consistently track your performance using tools like Google Analytics and Google Search Console to fine-tune your SEO efforts.

By mastering WordPress SEO and implementing these strategies, you'll be able to boost your website's visibility, attract more organic traffic, and ultimately grow your online presence.

Chapter 22: WordPress for E-Commerce: Building an Online Store

E-commerce has revolutionized the way businesses interact with customers, and WordPress has become one of the most popular platforms for building online stores. Powered by the **WooCommerce plugin**, WordPress allows anyone from small business owners to large enterprises to create fully functional e-commerce websites. This chapter will guide you through the essential steps to set up, manage, and optimize an e-commerce store using WooCommerce.

Introduction to WooCommerce

Why WooCommerce is the Go-To Plugin for WordPress E-Commerce

WooCommerce is the leading e-commerce plugin for WordPress, powering over 30% of all online stores worldwide. Its flexibility, scalability, and integration with WordPress make it the preferred solution for businesses of all sizes. WooCommerce provides a user-friendly interface, customizable options, and an extensive range of add-ons to extend functionality.

Key Features of WooCommerce:

- **Easy to Use**: WooCommerce seamlessly integrates with WordPress, allowing users to manage products, orders, and customers from a single dashboard.

- **Highly Customizable**: WooCommerce can be tailored to fit any business model, from physical stores to digital products or subscription-based services.

- **Extensive Extensions**: WooCommerce has a vast ecosystem of extensions, including payment gateways, shipping calculators, and inventory management tools.

Real-World Example: Setting Up a Basic E-Commerce Store Selling Products

To understand the power of WooCommerce, let's walk through setting up a basic online store. For example, suppose you're creating an online store to sell handmade candles.

1. **Installing WooCommerce**: Begin by installing the WooCommerce plugin via the WordPress dashboard. Follow the setup wizard to configure basic settings like currency, shipping methods, and payment gateways.

2. **Creating Products**: Add your handmade candles as products in WooCommerce, assigning relevant details such as prices, stock quantities, and images.

3. **Payment Gateway Integration**: Configure payment gateways such as PayPal, Stripe, or credit card payments for secure transactions.

4. **Launching Your Store**: Once the products and payment options are in place, your e-commerce store is ready for customers to browse and buy.

Product Management and Inventory

Creating and Managing Product Listings (Physical, Digital, and Variations)

WooCommerce allows you to sell a wide range of products, including physical goods, digital products, and variations of a single product (e.g., different sizes or colors). Proper product management is key to ensuring your store runs smoothly.

1. **Adding Physical Products**: To add a physical product, simply go to **Products > Add New**, then enter product details such as title, description, price, SKU (Stock Keeping Unit), and product images.
2. **Adding Digital Products**: For downloadable products like e-books or software, select the **Virtual** and **Downloadable** checkboxes. Upload the digital file and set the price.
3. **Product Variations**: If you have products with multiple options (e.g., a t-shirt available in different sizes and colors), you can create product variations. WooCommerce allows you to set unique prices, SKUs, and stock levels for each variation.

Real-World Example: Managing a Product Catalog and Setting Up Payment Gateways

Imagine you're setting up an online bookstore. Your product catalog includes physical books and e-books. To manage your product catalog:

- **Physical Books**: Add each book as a physical product with relevant details such as price, shipping dimensions, and stock levels.
- **E-books**: Create digital versions of your books, with downloadable files available upon purchase.

For payments, configure gateways like PayPal, which is popular for both physical and digital product transactions. WooCommerce offers several built-in payment integrations, or you can extend functionality using third-party plugins.

Customizing WooCommerce for Your Business

Adding Custom Product Attributes, Categories, and Advanced Product Options

WooCommerce allows you to customize the structure of your products to suit your business needs.

1. **Product Attributes**: These are characteristics of a product (e.g., size, color, material). Attributes help customers filter

and search for products more easily. You can set attributes globally (e.g., for all products) or individually (e.g., for specific product types).

> o **Real-World Example**: For a clothing store, you can create attributes like **Size** (Small, Medium, Large) and **Color** (Red, Blue, Black) to make it easier for customers to find what they're looking for.

2. **Product Categories**: Organizing products into categories helps customers navigate your store more easily. Categories can be hierarchical, meaning you can have parent and child categories (e.g., **Men's Clothing > Shirts > Casual Shirts**).

3. **Advanced Product Options**: For more complex customization, WooCommerce integrates with plugins like **WooCommerce Extra Product Options or Product Add-Ons** to allow customers to select additional options (e.g., engraving on jewelry or gift wrapping).

> o **Real-World Example**: A custom t-shirt shop could allow customers to upload their own images, select fonts, and add custom text to their shirts using product add-ons.

Real-World Example: Creating a Custom Product Page Layout for a Clothing Store

For a clothing store, you might want a custom product page layout to highlight key details, such as fabric type, size guides, and customer reviews. This can be achieved through the following steps:

- **Custom Fields**: Use plugins like **Advanced Custom Fields** to add extra fields for product details (e.g., **Material** or **Fit**).
- **Custom Layouts**: Create a custom template for product pages using a theme builder like **Elementor** or **WPBakery**.
- **Visual Elements**: Add high-quality product images, videos, and a size guide to improve the shopping experience.

Optimizing E-Commerce Performance

How to Optimize WooCommerce Stores for Speed and SEO

Performance optimization is essential for both user experience and SEO. A slow-loading site can lead to cart abandonment and reduced conversion rates.

1. **Caching**: Use caching plugins like **WP Rocket** or **W3 Total Cache** to reduce server load and speed up page loading times.
2. **Image Optimization**: Use plugins like **Smush** or **ShortPixel** to automatically compress product images without losing quality. This will improve load times, especially on product pages with multiple images.

3. **SEO for E-Commerce**: Implement SEO best practices such as optimizing product descriptions, using structured data, and ensuring mobile responsiveness. Plugins like **Yoast SEO** and **Rank Math** can help automate these tasks.

Real-World Example: Implementing Caching and Image Optimization for Faster Checkout

- **Caching**: Implement page caching so that product and category pages load instantly when visited by returning customers.
- **Image Optimization**: Ensure that all product images, including high-resolution images on product pages, are optimized to load quickly without compromising quality.

By improving site performance, you ensure that customers experience faster load times, resulting in reduced cart abandonment and increased sales.

---

s:

- WooCommerce is a powerful, customizable e-commerce solution for WordPress, allowing you to sell physical and digital products, as well as services.

- Product management involves adding detailed listings, managing inventory, and setting up payment gateways.
- You can further customize WooCommerce by adding attributes, categories, and advanced product options to fit your business model.
- Optimizing your WooCommerce store for speed and SEO is essential for improving user experience and ranking in search engines.
- Regularly update your store's functionality, performance, and marketing strategies to stay competitive in the ever-evolving e-commerce space.

By mastering WooCommerce, you can build a fully functioning online store that meets the needs of both your business and your customers, ensuring a seamless and profitable e-commerce experience.

Chapter 23: Scaling and Performance Optimization for WordPress

As your WordPress website grows, ensuring that it performs efficiently under increasing traffic becomes critical. Slow-loading pages, downtime, and performance bottlenecks can lead to poor user experience and a drop in SEO rankings. This chapter delves into various strategies and tools that can help you scale your WordPress site, optimize its performance, and provide a fast, reliable user experience.

Improving Website Speed and Performance

Techniques to Improve WordPress Performance: Caching, Image Compression, Lazy Loading

Speed is a key factor in both user experience and SEO. The faster your site loads, the better the experience for users, and the higher the chances of retaining visitors. The following techniques are essential for improving the performance of your WordPress website:

1. **Caching**:
   - **What is Caching?**: Caching is the process of storing copies of files or web pages so that they can

be accessed more quickly by users in the future, reducing the load on the server.

- o **Types of Caching**:
    - **Page Caching**: Stores static versions of dynamic pages, so users don't have to wait for the page to be generated each time.
    - **Browser Caching**: Stores static resources (images, stylesheets, JavaScript) in the user's browser for faster loading on repeat visits.
    - **Object Caching**: Stores the results of database queries to avoid repeated queries to the database, speeding up page load times.
- o **Tools for Caching**: Plugins like **W3 Total Cache** and **WP Rocket** can help implement various types of caching on your WordPress site.

2. **Image Compression**:
   - o **Why Image Optimization Matters**: Images often constitute a significant portion of a webpage's weight. Large, unoptimized images can slow down the page loading time.
   - o **Optimization Methods**:
       - **Lossless Compression**: Reduces file size without compromising quality.

- **Lossy Compression**: Reduces file size at the expense of some quality, often invisible to the human eye.
- **Tools**: Plugins like **Smush** or **ShortPixel** can automatically optimize images when they are uploaded, or bulk optimize images on your site.

3. **Lazy Loading**:

   o **What is Lazy Loading?**: Lazy loading defers the loading of images, videos, and other media files until the user scrolls down the page to them.

   o **Benefits**: This technique reduces the initial load time and saves bandwidth, especially on pages with large media files.

   o **Tools for Lazy Loading**: WordPress offers native lazy loading for images, but you can enhance it further with plugins like **a3 Lazy Load**.

Real-World Example: Speeding Up a Media-Heavy Site by Optimizing Images and Setting Up a Caching Plugin

Imagine you run a photography portfolio site with hundreds of high-resolution images. Visitors are complaining about slow page load times, and you've noticed a drop in traffic.

1. **Optimize Images**: You use the **Smush** plugin to automatically compress and resize images as they are

uploaded. For existing images, you run the bulk optimization tool.

2. **Set Up Caching**: Install **W3 Total Cache** and configure page caching, browser caching, and object caching. The caching plugin reduces server load by serving cached pages to returning visitors, improving load times.

3. **Enable Lazy Loading**: Enable WordPress's native lazy loading for images to ensure that media files load only when users scroll to them.

After implementing these techniques, your site's speed improves significantly, and user experience enhances, especially for mobile visitors.

Database Optimization and Cleanup

Importance of Database Optimization and Best Practices for Cleaning Up the Database

WordPress databases store all content, settings, and configurations for your website. Over time, databases can become bloated with unnecessary data, such as old post revisions, spam comments, and unused plugins. Optimizing and cleaning up your database can help reduce server load and improve site performance.

1. **Database Optimization**:

- o Regularly cleaning up and optimizing the WordPress database helps reduce overhead, keeping the database lean and efficient.
- o WordPress stores each draft of a post or page as a separate entry. Over time, this can accumulate a lot of unnecessary data.

2. **Best Practices for Database Cleanup**:
   - o **Delete Post Revisions**: WordPress saves multiple versions of a post or page (called revisions). These can be safely deleted once they are no longer needed.
   - o **Remove Unused Tables**: After deactivating plugins or themes, you may have leftover database tables that serve no purpose and can be deleted.
   - o **Clean Up Transients**: WordPress uses transients for caching data temporarily. However, expired transients can clutter the database.

Real-World Example: Using a Plugin to Optimize Database Tables and Remove Old Revisions

Let's say you've been blogging for years, and your WordPress site has become sluggish. After inspecting your database, you realize that there are thousands of post revisions and old drafts clogging up space.

1. **Install the WP-Optimize Plugin**: This plugin provides an easy way to clean up your database. You configure it to:
   - Remove post revisions older than a certain number of days.
   - Delete spam comments and trashed posts.
   - Clean expired transients from the database.

2. **Run Optimization**: Once configured, you run the database cleanup tool, reducing the size of the database and improving your site's speed.

Content Delivery Networks (CDN)

What is a CDN and Why It's Essential for Global Performance
A Content Delivery Network (CDN) is a network of geographically distributed servers that store cached versions of your site's content. When a user visits your website, the CDN serves content from the server nearest to them, reducing load times and improving the overall performance of your site.

Why Use a CDN?

- **Improved Site Speed**: By serving content from the closest server, the CDN reduces latency and speeds up the delivery of resources like images, CSS, and JavaScript.

- **Better User Experience**: Visitors from around the world experience faster load times, improving their interaction with your site.

- **Reduced Server Load**: By offloading static content to the CDN, your server doesn't need to handle every request, reducing its workload.

Real-World Example: Setting Up a CDN for a WordPress Site to Speed Up Content Delivery

You run a global blog with high-resolution images and videos, and your website is slow for international visitors. Here's how you can implement a CDN:

1. **Choose a CDN Provider**: Popular CDN providers for WordPress include **Cloudflare**, **KeyCDN**, and **MaxCDN**.

2. **Configure the CDN**: Install a CDN plugin like **W3 Total Cache** or **Cloudflare** for WordPress. Once configured, the CDN will cache static content and serve it from the nearest server to your visitors.

3. **Test Performance**: After activating the CDN, test the site's speed using tools like **GTMetrix** or **Pingdom** to confirm the improvement in load times.

Load Balancing and Server Scalability

Advanced Scaling Strategies for High-Traffic Websites, Including Load Balancing

When your website experiences high traffic, you need to ensure that it can handle the load. This is where **load balancing** comes into play.

1. **What is Load Balancing?**
    - Load balancing distributes incoming traffic across multiple servers to ensure no single server is overwhelmed.
    - Load balancers can be hardware-based or software-based and are used to distribute both HTTP and HTTPS traffic efficiently.

2. **Server Scalability**:
    - **Vertical Scaling**: Increasing the resources (RAM, CPU) of a single server.
    - **Horizontal Scaling**: Adding more servers to distribute traffic.

Real-World Example: Configuring a WordPress Site on Cloud Hosting with Auto-Scaling

Suppose your WordPress blog has gained massive popularity, and your single server can no longer handle the traffic load. Here's how you can scale:

1. **Cloud Hosting Setup**: You migrate your WordPress site to a cloud provider like **Amazon Web Services (AWS)**, **Google Cloud**, or **DigitalOcean**.

2. **Set Up Load Balancer**: Use an **AWS Elastic Load Balancer** or a similar service to distribute traffic across multiple web servers.

3. **Enable Auto-Scaling**: Set up **auto-scaling** rules to automatically add or remove servers based on traffic demand.

4. **Optimize Database and Caching**: To further optimize, configure database replication and use a CDN to offload static content.

---

s:

- Improving WordPress performance involves using caching, image compression, and lazy loading to speed up the website and enhance the user experience.

- Regular database optimization and cleanup are crucial for reducing bloat and improving performance.

- CDNs are essential for speeding up content delivery, especially for global audiences, by serving cached versions of content from the nearest server.

- Load balancing and server scalability are important strategies for handling high traffic and ensuring that your WordPress site remains responsive under load.

By implementing these performance optimization techniques, you can scale your WordPress website to handle increasing traffic while delivering a fast, reliable, and high-quality user experience.

Chapter 24: WordPress Multisite and Managing Multiple Websites

WordPress Multisite is a powerful feature that allows you to manage multiple WordPress websites from a single WordPress installation. This feature is especially useful for organizations, businesses, or individuals who need to maintain a network of sites—whether it's for a group of blogs, a multi-location business, or an educational institution with several departments. This chapter will guide you through the benefits, setup, and management of a WordPress Multisite network, along with best practices for maintaining security, performance, and user roles across multiple sites.

Understanding WordPress Multisite

What is WordPress Multisite and How It Can Help Manage Multiple Sites from One Dashboard

WordPress Multisite enables you to create and manage multiple websites from a single WordPress installation. Instead of installing a separate instance of WordPress for each site, you can run a network of sites from one central dashboard, making site management more efficient and streamlined.

1. **Key Features of WordPress Multisite**:

- o **Single WordPress Installation**: You only need to install WordPress once. After setting up Multisite, you can add as many websites as you need.

- o **Centralized Management**: Manage themes, plugins, users, and settings from a single dashboard, making administration much simpler for large networks.

- o **Subdomains or Subdirectories**: You can choose to set up your sites as subdomains (e.g., site1.yourdomain.com) or subdirectories (e.g., yourdomain.com/site1).

2. **When to Use WordPress Multisite**:

- o **Franchises**: Manage a network of websites for different locations under one dashboard.

- o **Educational Institutions**: Provide different departments with their own sub-sites but manage everything centrally.

- o **Community Websites**: Set up a platform where users can create their own websites within the network (such as a blog network).

Real-World Example: Setting Up a Network of Sites for a Franchise or Educational Institution

Imagine a restaurant franchise with multiple branches in different cities. Each location needs a unique website, but the corporate team wants to manage all sites from one dashboard.

1. **Setting Up Multisite**: The corporate WordPress site is set up with Multisite enabled. Each franchise location gets a sub-site (e.g., location1.franchise.com, location2.franchise.com).

2. **Managing Content**: The central dashboard allows the corporate team to oversee content updates, plugin installations, and security settings for each franchise location's site.

With WordPress Multisite, the corporate team can easily manage all locations from one centralized dashboard without needing to log into multiple WordPress instances.

Managing Themes and Plugins in Multisite

Centralized Theme and Plugin Management in a Multisite Environment

In a multisite network, managing themes and plugins can be more efficient since they can be installed and managed centrally. Instead of installing the same theme or plugin on every individual site, you can install them once, and make them available to all sites in the network.

1. **Themes**:

WORDPRESS DEVELOPMENT GUIDE

- o **Network-Enabled Themes**: Once a theme is installed and network-enabled, you can choose which sites can use it. You can also prevent individual site admins from adding their own themes.
- o **Managing Theme Updates**: You only need to update a theme once for it to apply across all sites in the network.

2. **Plugins**:
- o **Network-Activated Plugins**: Similar to themes, once a plugin is activated across the network, it will be available to all sites. You can also choose which plugins to activate on specific sites within the network.
- o **Plugin Compatibility**: Some plugins may only be compatible with WordPress Multisite, so it's essential to check for compatibility before installing them.

Real-World Example: Installing a Plugin for All Sites in a Multisite Network

Suppose you want to install a SEO plugin across all sites in your multisite network:

1. **Install and Network-Activate the Plugin**: You install a plugin like **Yoast SEO** and activate it across the network.

2. **Configuring the Plugin for Each Site**: Although the plugin is activated on all sites, you can still configure individual settings for each site to suit its content.

By network-activating plugins like SEO or caching plugins, you can ensure consistency and better management of all the sites within the network.

User Management and Permissions in Multisite

Managing Users, Roles, and Permissions Across Multiple Sites
In WordPress Multisite, you can create users who have access to different sites in the network. You can assign roles and permissions to users at both the network level and the individual site level.

1. **Roles in Multisite**:
   - o **Super Admin**: This is the highest level of access and can manage the entire network.
   - o **Site Admin**: A user who has administrative access to a specific site within the network but does not have control over the entire multisite installation.
   - o **Contributor/Editor**: Users who can create and manage content, but their access is limited to specific sites.

o **Subscriber**: Users who can only view content.

2. **Granting Access to Certain Subsites While Restricting Permissions**:

   o **Network Users**: You can add users at the network level (e.g., users who should have access to multiple sites).

   o **Site-Specific Users**: You can add users specifically to a single site in the network with appropriate permissions.

   o **Role Customization**: You can customize user roles within each site to control permissions on a granular level.

Real-World Example: Granting Access to Certain Subsites While Restricting Permissions

Imagine an educational institution using Multisite where different departments (e.g., Math, History, Art) need separate sites but with different levels of user access:

1. **Math Department**: You set up a site for the Math Department and assign a faculty member as the Site Admin. Students can be contributors, able to post content but not manage the site.

2. **History Department**: Faculty members in the History Department have administrative access, but student assistants only have editing access.

3. **Restrict Access to Other Sites**: You ensure that users in the History Department cannot access or modify content in the Math Department's site.

By managing user roles and permissions, you ensure that each department has the right level of access to their site without cross-site interference.

Best Practices for Multisite Management

Maintaining Security and Performance Across a Network of WordPress Sites

Managing a network of sites comes with its own set of challenges, particularly with security and performance. Keeping the entire network secure and performing optimally requires diligent planning and best practices.

1. **Security Best Practices**:
   o **Regular Backups**: Backup the entire multisite network regularly. A failure in one subsite can affect the entire network.
   o **Enforcing Strong Passwords**: Use a plugin to enforce strong password policies for all users.

- o **Two-Factor Authentication**: For added security, enable two-factor authentication (2FA) for site admins.

- o **Limit Plugin Installations**: Limit the number of plugins that users can install to prevent performance issues and potential security risks.

2. **Performance Optimization**:

- o **Database Optimization**: Keep your database optimized by regularly cleaning up post revisions, spam comments, and unused tables.

- o **Caching**: Implement caching at both the network level and individual sites to speed up performance.

- o **CDN Integration**: Use a Content Delivery Network (CDN) to serve static assets like images and CSS files more quickly.

Real-World Example: Backing Up a Multisite Network and Setting Up Update Policies

You are managing a WordPress multisite network for an organization with 50 sub-sites. You need to ensure that the network is secure and the performance is optimal.

1. **Backup Strategy**: You implement a regular backup schedule using a plugin like **UpdraftPlus** or **BackupBuddy**, ensuring that the entire network is backed up regularly.

2. **Update Policies**: Set up automatic plugin and theme updates for the entire network, but manually approve major updates or new installations to ensure compatibility across all sites.

---

s:

- **WordPress Multisite** is ideal for managing multiple websites from a single WordPress installation, reducing the overhead of managing separate sites.

- **Centralized management of themes and plugins** allows for more efficient updates and configuration across all sites in the network.

- **User management** in Multisite provides granular control over permissions, ensuring that users have appropriate access to specific sites within the network.

- **Best practices for multisite management** include regular backups, security measures, and performance optimizations to maintain a secure and fast-running network.

By implementing these strategies and using the power of WordPress Multisite, you can effectively manage a large network of websites with minimal hassle.

Chapter 25: Future Trends in WordPress Development

WordPress has been one of the most popular content management systems (CMS) for over a decade, powering more than 40% of all websites on the internet. As web technologies continue to evolve, WordPress is adapting to meet the growing demands of developers and website owners. In this chapter, we will explore the future of WordPress development, including new trends and technologies that will shape the platform in the coming years. We'll look into the WordPress REST API, headless WordPress, the Jamstack architecture, and the emerging role of artificial intelligence (AI) and machine learning in WordPress development.

The Evolution of WordPress

Overview of the Future of WordPress as a Content Management System

WordPress has come a long way from its beginnings as a simple blogging platform. Today, it's a powerful CMS used by everyone from small bloggers to large enterprises. As the web continues to change, so too does WordPress. The future of WordPress lies in its ability to adapt to new technologies, improve user experience, and continue supporting developers in creating modern, high-performance websites.

1. **Key Trends in WordPress Development**:
   - o **Mobile-First Approach**: As mobile traffic continues to grow, WordPress will place even more emphasis on creating responsive, mobile-friendly websites. Themes and plugins will continue to evolve with this mobile-first philosophy in mind.
   - o **Faster Performance**: With a push toward performance optimization, WordPress will improve its default features to ensure faster loading times, including better caching systems, improved database management, and integration with Content Delivery Networks (CDNs).
   - o **User Experience**: WordPress will focus on improving the user interface and user experience (UI/UX) for both website owners and developers. Tools like the **Block Editor** (Gutenberg) are pushing the platform toward a more intuitive, visual experience.

2. **Modern Web Technologies**:
   - o **Integration with JavaScript Frameworks**: The evolution of WordPress toward a more flexible and developer-friendly platform will see better

integration with modern JavaScript frameworks like **React**, **Vue.js**, and **Angular**.

o **Headless WordPress**: WordPress is moving beyond its traditional role as a content management system by enabling headless architecture, where WordPress serves as the back-end content source while the front-end can be developed using any framework or technology.

How WordPress is Adapting to Modern Web Technologies and Trends (e.g., Headless WordPress)

WordPress is evolving to become more than just a traditional CMS, allowing developers to build dynamic, customized websites using modern tools. Headless WordPress is one of the most significant changes in recent years, allowing WordPress to function as the back-end content management system while decoupling the front-end to use technologies like React or Vue.js.

- **Benefits of Headless WordPress**:
    - o **Flexibility**: You can use any front-end technology, making it ideal for custom web applications, mobile apps, and other digital experiences.
    - o **Performance**: By decoupling the front-end and back-end, you can improve site performance, as the front-end can be optimized separately.

o **Omnichannel Capabilities**: Headless WordPress makes it easier to publish content across multiple platforms, such as websites, mobile apps, and even IoT devices.

The Role of REST API and Headless WordPress

Introduction to the WordPress REST API and Its Use Cases

The **WordPress REST API** is a game-changer for WordPress development. It allows developers to interact with WordPress programmatically, enabling the integration of WordPress with external applications, systems, or services. The REST API makes it possible to build headless websites and mobile apps that use WordPress as the back-end content manager.

1. **What is the REST API?**

   o The WordPress REST API provides developers with a way to retrieve data from a WordPress site or interact with the site's features via HTTP requests. It exposes WordPress data, such as posts, pages, users, and more, in JSON format, making it easy to integrate with other systems and front-end technologies.

2. **Use Cases for the REST API**:

- o **Building Custom Front-End Applications**: Developers can use frameworks like React, Vue.js, or Angular to build a custom front-end that interacts with WordPress via the REST API.

- o **Mobile App Integration**: The REST API allows WordPress to serve as the content management system for mobile apps, providing real-time updates to app content.

- o **Third-Party Integrations**: You can integrate WordPress with third-party services like CRM systems, email marketing platforms, and e-commerce tools using the API.

Real-World Example: Using the WordPress API to Create a Custom Front-End Application

Let's say you're building a dynamic web app for a news website. You want to keep WordPress as your content management system, but you need more flexibility in how the content is displayed.

1. **Step 1: Set Up the WordPress REST API**: Ensure the REST API is enabled and accessible on your WordPress site.

2. **Step 2: Build the Front-End with React**: You build a front-end application using React, fetching data from WordPress via the REST API. You can display posts, categories, and custom post types as needed.

3. **Step 3: Connect the Back-End and Front-End**: The React app interacts with WordPress to retrieve content, update posts, or display comments. The two systems are now decoupled but still work together seamlessly.

WordPress and the Jamstack Architecture

What is Jamstack, and Why It's Becoming Popular with WordPress Developers

Jamstack (JavaScript, APIs, and Markup) is an architecture that focuses on decoupling the front-end from the back-end, enabling faster, more secure, and scalable websites. Jamstack sites are built with static files generated from dynamic content sources. This architecture is becoming increasingly popular with WordPress developers, particularly for building high-performance websites.

1. **How Jamstack Benefits WordPress Development**:
   o **Performance**: By serving pre-rendered static files, Jamstack sites load faster, leading to a better user experience.
   o **Scalability**: Static files can be served from CDNs, making them easier to scale as traffic grows.
   o **Security**: Static sites are less vulnerable to attacks because there's no database or server-side code running on the client side.

2. **WordPress as a Headless CMS for Jamstack**:

   o WordPress can be used as the content source for Jamstack sites. WordPress handles content management while static site generators (like Gatsby or Hugo) handle the front-end rendering, pulling data from WordPress via the REST API or GraphQL.

Real-World Example: Building a Static Site Using WordPress as the Backend

Let's say you want to build a blog that serves static HTML files for faster performance, but you want to keep WordPress as the content management system.

1. **Step 1: Set Up WordPress as a Headless CMS**: Use the REST API or GraphQL to fetch posts, pages, and custom content types.

2. **Step 2: Generate Static Pages with a Static Site Generator**: Use a tool like **Gatsby** to pull content from the WordPress site and generate static HTML pages.

3. **Step 3: Deploy to a CDN**: Once the site is generated, deploy it to a CDN like Netlify or Vercel for fast global distribution.

Emerging Technologies and WordPress

The Role of AI, Machine Learning, and Automation in WordPress Development

Emerging technologies like **artificial intelligence (AI)**, **machine learning**, and **automation** are becoming increasingly influential in web development, including WordPress. These technologies have the potential to enhance the user experience, improve SEO, automate content creation, and optimize website performance.

1. **AI-Powered Content Creation**:
    - AI tools like **WordLift** or **INK for All** are helping WordPress site owners optimize their content for SEO and automate tasks like keyword research and content suggestions.

2. **Machine Learning for Personalization**:
    - Machine learning algorithms can analyze user behavior and serve personalized content, such as recommending products or articles based on past interactions.

3. **Automated Workflows and Plugins**:
    - Plugins like **Zapier** or **Automate.io** are allowing WordPress users to automate tasks like content publishing, social media sharing, and email marketing, reducing manual effort and increasing efficiency.

Real-World Example: Using AI-Driven Tools to Optimize Content Creation and SEO

Consider a small business owner using WordPress to manage their website. They want to improve their SEO but don't have the time or expertise to manually optimize every piece of content.

1. **AI Tools for SEO Optimization**: Using an AI-powered tool like **RankMath** or **Yoast SEO**, the site can automatically suggest keywords, improve metadata, and optimize page content for search engines.

2. **AI Content Generation**: The business owner uses AI-powered content creation tools to generate blog posts based on targeted keywords, streamlining the content production process.

---

s:

- WordPress is continuously evolving to embrace modern web technologies, including headless WordPress, the REST API, and the Jamstack architecture.
- The **WordPress REST API** allows developers to build custom front-end applications and integrate WordPress with third-party services.

- The **Jamstack architecture** leverages WordPress as a back-end CMS for static site generation, offering performance, scalability, and security benefits.
- Emerging technologies like **AI** and **machine learning** are enhancing WordPress development, optimizing SEO, automating tasks, and personalizing content for users.

As WordPress continues to evolve and adopt cutting-edge technologies, developers can look forward to a platform that is more flexible, scalable, and developer-friendly than ever before.

www.ingramcontent.com/pod-product-compliance
Lightning Source LLC
LaVergne TN
LVHW022341060326
832902LV00022B/4173